SOCIAL STUDIES

Anthology

WITH TEACHING STRATEGIES

THE WORLD AROUND US

The wonderful variety of United States regions is clear in the cover photos—from the Native American cave painting in Utah to the cornfields of the Middle West, the towering skyscrapers of New York City, and the desert of Monument Valley in Arizona.

MACMILLAN/McGRAW-HILL SCHOOL PUBLISHING COMPANY

NEW YORK   CHICAGO   COLUMBUS

PROGRAM AUTHORS •

Dr. James A. Banks
Professor of Education and Director of the Center for
   Multicultural Education
University of Washington
Seattle, Washington

Dr. Barry K. Beyer
Professor of Education and American Studies
George Mason University
Fairfax, Virginia

Dr. Gloria Contreras
Professor of Education and Director of the Office of
   Multicultural Affairs
University of North Texas
Denton, Texas

Jean Craven
District Coordinator of Curriculum Development
Albuquerque Public Schools
Albuquerque, New Mexico

Dr. Gloria Ladson-Billings
Assistant Professor of Education
University of Wisconsin
Madison, Wisconsin

Dr. Mary A. McFarland
Director of Staff Development and Instructional
   Coordinator of Social Studies, K-12
Parkway School District
Chesterfield, Missouri

Dr. Walter C. Parker
Associate Professor of Social Studies Education and
   Director of the Center for the Study of Civic
   Intelligence
University of Washington
Seattle, Washington

CONTENT CONSULTANTS •

Yvonne Beamer
Resource Specialist
Native American Education Program
New York, New York

Mario T. Garcia
Professor of History and American Studies
Yale University
New Haven, Connecticut

Valerie Ooka Pang
Associate Professor, School of Teacher Education
San Diego State University
San Diego, California

Clifford E. Trafzer
Professor of Ethnic Studies and Director of Native
   American Studies
University of California
Riverside, California

GRADE-LEVEL CONSULTANTS •

Virginia Moore Bryant
Teacher of Gifted Students
Pascagoula Municipal Separate School District
Pascagoula, Mississippi

Nancy Blye
Elementary Teacher
Kendale Lakes Elementary School
Miami, Florida

Kathy Hellesen
Elementary Teacher
Hoover School
Schaumburg, Illinois

Cherrye Fincher Shepard
Elementary Teacher
Central Park Elementary
Birmingham, Alabama

ACKNOWLEDGMENTS •

*The publisher gratefully acknowledges permission to reprint
the following copyrighted material:*

"The Heavy Pants of Mr. Strauss" from THE SPICE OF
AMERICA by June Swanson. Text copyright © 1983 by
June Swanson. Published by Carolrhoda Books, Inc.,
Minneapolis, MN. Used with permission. All rights
reserved.

Excerpt (Ch. 4) from GO FREE OR DIE: *A Story about
Harriet Tubman* by Jeri Ferris. Text copyright © 1988 by
Jeri Ferris. Published by Carolrhoda Books, Inc.,
Minneapolis, MN. Used with permission. All rights
reserved.

(continued on page 166)

TABLE OF *Contents*

= audio cassette

USING YOUR *Anthology*

In *Regions Near and Far* you will be reading about many different people, places, and times. This Anthology, or collection of documents created by different people, will make the information in your textbook come to life in a special way. The Anthology includes stories, songs, poems, diaries, and even old advertisements and posters. As you read and study these documents, you will be able to see, feel, and hear what it is like to live in other places. Your Anthology will even take you back into the past and help you feel what it was like to live in other times! The selections in your Anthology will help you to better understand life in diverse regions of the United States, both past and present.

CASSETTE LOGO •
Tells you that the selection appears on the Anthology Cassette

TEXTBOOK LINK •
Tells you which chapter and lesson in your textbook the document is linked to

CONCLUSION •
Tells you what happened next and asks you to think further about the selection

INTRODUCTION •
Gives you background information about the selection and tells you what kind of document it is. Is it fiction or nonfiction? Is it a poem or a song? The introduction also asks you a question to think about as you read the document.

DEFINITIONS •
Gives you the meanings of difficult words

SOURCE •
Tells you where the selection came from

Use with Chapter 3, Lesson 1

THE NEW COLOSSUS

by Emma Lazarus, 1883

When France gave the United States the Statue of Liberty as a gift in 1880, Emma Lazarus was moved to write the poem, The New Colossus. A colossus is something gigantic. Emma Lazarus was born in New York City in 1849. As a young woman, she saw both her city and the United States change with the constant flow of immigrants from other countries. Many arrived penniless, carrying just a bundle of clothing. But they also came with great dreams of starting a new life in a new land. Who is the Statue of Liberty welcoming?

Not like the **brazen** giant of Greek fame,
With **conquering** limbs **astride** from land to land;
Here at our sea-washed, sunset gates shall stand
A mighty woman with a torch, whose flame
Is the **imprisoned** lightning, and her name
Mother of **Exiles**. From her **beacon-hand**
Glows world-wide welcome; her mild eyes command
The air-bridged harbor that twin cities frame.

"Keep, ancient lands, your **storied pomp**!" cries she
With silent lips. "Give me your tired, your poor,
Your **huddled masses** yearning to breathe free,
The **wretched refuse** of your **teeming** shore.
Send these, the homeless, **tempest-tost** to me,
I lift my lamp beside the golden door!"

brazen: bold
conquering: mighty
astride: with one leg on each side

imprisoned: captured
exiles: people forced out of their countries
beacon-hand: hand that holds a guiding light
storied pomp: old habits and fancy ways
huddled masses: crowds of poor people
wretched refuse: unwanted people
teeming: crowded
tempest-tost: battered by storms

The New Colossus was carved into a bronze plaque and mounted at the base of the Statue of Liberty when the statue was completed in 1886. Today, the statue still welcomes people coming to the United States through New York Harbor. The statue symbolizes hope and freedom to millions of people throughout the world.

Source: Emma Lazarus, *Poems of Emma Lazarus.* Boston: Houghton-Mifflin Company, 1889.

26

UNIT 1

STUDYING REGIONS

Give me your tired, your poor, Your huddled masses yearning to breathe free.

from "The New Colossus"
by Emma Lazarus

Sincerely, Samantha

by Samantha Smith and Yuri Andropov, 1982

Having a pen pal is a great way to learn about other places. Sometimes a letter can help to change the world! In November 1982 a fifth-grade girl named Samantha Smith of Manchester, Maine, was reading a newspaper article with her mother. The article troubled Samantha. It was about the possibility of nuclear war between the United States and the Soviet Union. Samantha was confused and worried. Why would two countries that wanted peace end up in war? She decided to write a letter to the leader of the Soviet Union, Yuri Andropov, and ask him herself.

Dear Mr. Andropov,

My name is Samantha Smith. I am ten years old. Congratulations on your new job. I have been worrying about Russia and the United States getting into a nuclear war. Are you going to vote to have a war or not? If you aren't please tell me how you are going to help to not have a war. This question you do not have to answer, but I would like to know why you want to conquer the world or at least our country. God made the world for us to live together in peace and not to fight.

Sincerely,
Samantha Smith

Five months passed and Samantha Smith forgot about the letter she had sent. Little did she know that a newspaper in the Soviet Union, Pravda, had already printed a copy of her letter, and a response from Andropov was in the mail to her. The day she received the response a crowd of reporters greeted her on her lawn after school. Here is part of the letter she received.

Samantha SMITH
Manchester, Maine   USA

Dear Samantha,

I received your letter, as well as many others coming to me these days from your country, and from other countries in the world.

It seems to me . . . that you are a **courageous** and honest girl, **resembling** Tom Sawyer's friend from the well-known book of your **compatriot Mark Twain**. All kids in our country—boys and girls alike—know and love this book.

You write that you are worried about our two countries going into a nuclear war, and you ask whether we can do something to prevent it.

Yes, Samantha, we in the Soviet Union are trying to do every-thing so that there will not be war between our two countries, so that there will be no war at all on Earth. This is the wish of everyone in the Soviet Union. . . .

No one in our country—neither workers, peasants, writers nor doctors, neither grown-ups nor children, nor members of the government—wants either a big or "little" war.

We want peace. . . . We are occupied with growing wheat, building and inventing, writing books and flying into space. We want peace for ourselves and for all peoples of the planet. For our children and for you, Samantha.

I invite you, if your parents will let you, to come to our country, the best time being the summer. You will find out about our country. . . . And see for yourself: in the Soviet Union every-one is for peace and friendship among peoples.

Thank you for your letter. I wish you all the best in your young life.

Yuri Andropov

courageous: brave
resembling: like

compatriot: fellow citizen
Mark Twain: an American author who lived in the 1800s.

Samantha accepted Yuri Andropov's invitation to visit the Soviet Union. People everywhere hoped her trip would be the beginning of friendship between the two countries. Following her trip Samantha gave speeches and traveled to other states and countries talking about the need for world peace— and what children can do to make a difference. In 1985, when Samantha was only 13 years old, she and her father died in a plane crash. The Soviet Union issued a special postage stamp in her honor, which you can see on the top of page 2. Why do you think they chose to honor her with a stamp?

NO STAR NIGHTS

by Anna Egan Smucker

In the 1930s and 1940s, there were hundreds of steel mills in Ohio, Pennsylvania, and West Virginia. This area has always been rich in natural resources, especially in coal, the raw materials used for making steel. In her book No Star Nights, Anna Egan Smucker remembers what it was like to be a child in the mill town of Weirton, West Virginia. Smucker's father operated a crane in the steel mill. As you read this selection, notice how she recalls some memories that are fun, some that are painful, and some that are a little of both. How does the use of natural resources affect life in Weirton?

When I was little, we couldn't see the stars in the nighttime sky because the furnaces of the mill turned the darkness into a red glow. But we would lie on the hill and look up at the sky anyway and wait for a bright orange light that seemed to breathe in and out to spread across it. And we would know that the golden spark-spitting steel was being poured out of giant buckets into molds to cool.

Then we would look down on a train pulling cars mounted with giant **thimbles** rocking back and forth. They were filled with fiery hot **molten slag** that in the night glowed orange. And when they were dumped, the sky lit up again.

A loud steam whistle that echoed off the hills announced the change of shifts, and hundreds of men streamed out of the

thimbles: caps
molten: melted
slag: leftover materials

mill's gates. Everyone's dad worked in the mill, and carried a
tin lunch box and a big metal thermos bottle.

Work at the mill went on night and day. When Dad worked
night shift, we children had to whisper and play quietly during
the day so that we didn't wake him up. His job was too dangerous for him to go without sleep. He operated a crane that lifted
heavy **ingots** of steel into a pit that was thousands of degrees
hot.

ingots: bars of metal

When Dad worked the **three-to-eleven** shift, Mom made
dinner early so we could all eat together. She made the best
stuffed cabbage of anyone in the neighborhood. We sometimes
tried to help fold the cabbage leaves around the meat and rice
like she did, but our cabbage leaves always came unrolled.

three-to-eleven: 3:00
P.M. to 11:00 P.M.

During the school year days went by when we didn't see
Dad at all because he was either at work or sleeping. When he
changed shifts from daylight to night and back again it took
him a while to get used to the different waking and sleeping
times. We called these his grumpy times. We liked it best when
he had daylight hours to spend with us. We played baseball
until it was too dark to see the ball.

On a few very special summer afternoons he would load
us all into the car for a hot, sweaty trip to Pittsburgh and a

double header Pirates game at Forbes Field. We sat in the bleachers way out in left field, eating popcorn and drinking lemonade that we brought from home, yelling our heads off for the Pirates. Our brother always wore his baseball glove, hoping to catch a foul ball that might come into the stands. Dad helped us mark our scorecards and bought us hot dogs during the seventh-inning stretch.

On our way home we passed the black **silhouettes** of Pittsburgh's steel mills with their great heavy clouds of smoke **billowing** from endless rows of smokestacks. The road wound along as the river wound and between us and the river were the mills and on the other side of the road were the hills—the river, the mills, and the hills. And we sang as we rode home. "She'll be comin' round the mountain when she comes...."

silhouettes: outlines

billowing: blowing

We went to school across from the mill. The smokestacks towered above us and the smoke billowed out in great puffy clouds of red, orange, and yellow, but mostly the color of rust. Everything—houses, hedges, old cars—was a rusty red color. Everything but the little bits of **graphite** and they glinted like silver in the dust. At recess when the wind whirled these sharp shiny metal pieces around, we girls would crouch so that our skirts touched the ground and kept our bare legs from being stung.

graphite: a soft gray mineral

We would squint our eyes when the wind blew to keep the graphite out. Once a piece got caught in my eye and no matter how much I blinked or how much my eye watered it wouldn't come out. When the eye doctor finally took it out and showed kit to me I was amazed that a speck that small could feel so big.

We played on the steep street that ran up the hill beside our school. Our favorite game was dodge ball. The kids on the bottom row knew they had to catch the ball. If they didn't, it would roll down onto the busy county road that ran in front of the school. Too often a truck carrying a heavy roll of steel would run over it and with a loud bang the ball would be flattened.

The windows in our school were kept closed to try to keep the graphite and smoke out. On really windy days we could hear the dry, dusty sound of grit hitting against the glass.

Dusting the room was a daily job. The best duster got to dust the teacher's desk with a soft white cloth and a spray that made the whole room smell like lemons. It was always a mystery to us how the nuns who were our teachers could keep the white parts of their **habits** so clean. . . .

habits: nuns' clothing

The road we took home from school went right through part of the mill. Tall cement walls with strands of barbed wire at the top kept us on the sidewalk and out of the mill. But when we got to the bridge that spanned the railroad tracks, there was just a steel mesh fence. From there we could look straight down into the mill! There was always something wonderful to watch. Through a huge open doorway we could see the **mammoth open-hearth** furnace. A giant **ladle** would tilt to give the fiery furnace a "drink" of orange, molten iron. Sometimes we would see the golden liquid steel pouring out the bottom of the open hearth into enormous bucketlike ladles. The workers were just small dark figures made even smaller by the great size of the ladles and the furnace. The hot glow of the liquid steel made the dark mill light up as if the sun itself was being poured out. And standing on the bridge we could feel its awful heat. . . .

mammoth: huge
open-hearth: open at the front
ladle: spoon

Many years have passed since. . . . The night sky is clear and star filled because the mill is shut down. The big buckets no longer pour the hot, yellow steel. The furnaces whose fires lit up everything are rusting and cold.

Not many children live in the town now. Most of the younger people have moved away to other places to find work. The valley's steelworking way of life is gone forever. But whenever the grandchildren come back to visit they love more than anything else to listen to stories about the days when all night long the sky glowed red.

Just as in Smucker's story, many steel mills in the area have closed down. What things seem sad about the closing of the mills? What things seem better?

Source: Anna Egan Smucker, *No Star Nights*. New York: Knopf, 1989.

STATES AND CAPITALS

by Professor Rap

As you know our country is made up of 50 states. Each of these states has something special about it, and each state has a capital city where the state's government is located. Have you ever tried to memorize all of the states and their capitals? It's not an easy job. Professor Rap is a singer whose rap songs make learning Social Studies fun. How does Professor Rap use rhymes to teach the states and their capitals in the rap song below?

You got to learn, and get an education
Learn the states and capitals of our nation
We'll help you learn, border-to-border
So we'll start in alphabetical order
Alabama . . . in the south and summery
Its capital rhymes . . . Montgomery
In Alaska, there's always snow
Capital city . . . Juneau
It's easy to learn if you associate a rhyme
So let's keep it going, you're doing fine
It's pretty easy . . . pretty good
You kind of like it? . . . I knew you would

Arizona's is Phoenix . . . home of the cactus
This you will learn . . . with some practice
Little Rock's the capital of Arkansas
Now did you see who we just saw. . .
In California (Totally!) at the state's capital
Sacramento (Dude!) pretty radical
Colorado's capital is Denver
Heard the mountains are nice, but
 never been there
It's pretty easy . . . pretty good
You kind of like it? . . . I knew you would

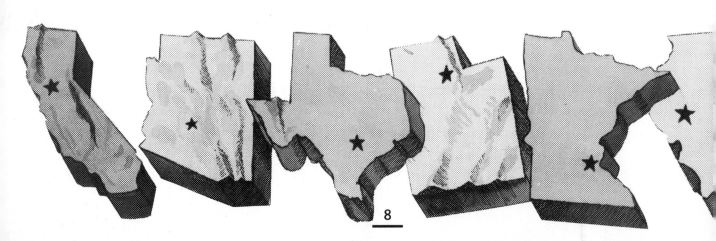

Hartford's the capital . . . of Connecticut
Sit up straight . . . it's proper etiquette
Delaware's capital . . . is Dover
Red Rover, Red Rover, send Billy right over
Florida, capital . . . Tallahassee
Lots of oranges, vitamin C
Atlanta is the capital of Georgia
Pay attention . . . we won't bore ya
Hawaii, capital . . . Honolulu
Tropical paradise, ocean blue
(ocean blue) . . . pretty good
You kind of like it? . . . I knew you would
It's pretty easy . . . pretty good
Boise's the capital of Idaho
Farmer Jack, getting busy growing . . .
    potatoes
Springfield's the capital of Illinois
Get up everybody, let's make some noise
In Indiana, cars go real fast
In the capital city of Indianapolis
Iowa's capital . . . is Des Moines
If you're not rappin' now, would you
    care to join?

Topeka . . . capital of Kansas
Walkin' the yellow brick road, you'll
    take some chances
It's pretty easy . . . pretty good
You kind of like it? . . . I knew you would
Frankfort's the capital of Kentucky
Finger lickin' good, let's get funky
Louisiana's capital is Baton Rouge
Hard to miss, the state is shaped like a boot
Augusta is the capital of Maine
And its lobsters are their claim-to-fame
Annapolis . . . the capital of Maryland
At the Naval Academy . . . boys
    become men
It's pretty easy . . . pretty good
You kind of like it? . . . I knew you would
Massachusetts' is Boston . . . raised the
    tax on the tea
The people didn't like it, threw it in the sea
Michigan's capital . . . is Lansing
Woods and lakes . . . hunting and fishing
Minnesota, capital . . . St. Paul
All for one, and one for all

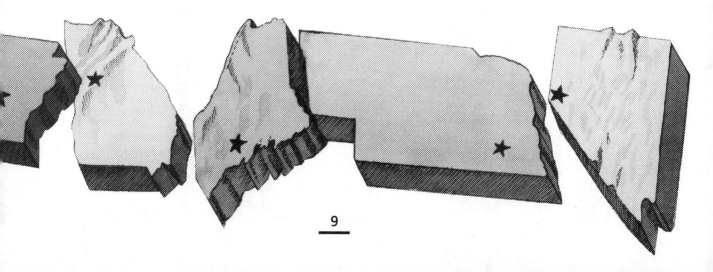

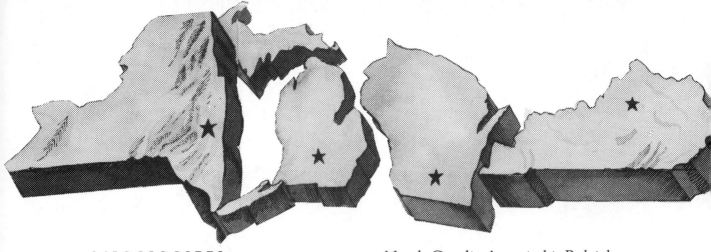

M-I-S-S-I-S-S-I-P-P-I
Jackson, Mississippi, where rivers run wide
Half way there . . . no need to worry
(Break down): G-G-G-Get down
Professor Rap's rocking the mike to a
   new sound
(Repeat and add groove)
The Continental Divide is in Montana
And the capital city is Helena
Nebraska is the Cornhusker State
Lincoln is the capital, keep up the pace
Nevada, capital . . . Carson City
Not learning your capitals would be a pity
New Hampshire, capital . . . Concord
Keep singing this rhyme 'cause you're
   not getting bored
Trenton is the capital . . . of New Jersey
A beautiful state set beside the sea
New Mexico . . . an enchanting place
And its capital city is Santa Fe
It's pretty easy . . . pretty good
You kind of like it? . . . I knew you would
New York . . . America's "Melting Pot"
Albany's its capital in case you forgot

North Carolina's capital is Raleigh
If you do good, you may get a lolly "POP!"
Bismarck's the capital of North Dakota
Home to the Sioux, and did you
   know that . . .
The Buckeye State is Ohio
The capital's Columbus, so let's go. . .
To Oklahoma . . . a-do-wah-ditty
Capital's simple . . . Oklahoma City
It's pretty easy . . . pretty good
You kind of like it? . . . I knew you would
Oregon's capital . . . is Salem
Guess what? (WHAT?) we're almost done
Pennsylvania . . . producer of steel
Harrisburg's the capital, these facts are
   for real
It's pretty easy . . . pretty good
You kind of like it? . . . I knew you would
Rhode Island's capital is Providence,
   it's evident
One of the 13 colonies to achieve
   independence
Let's go . . . to South Carolina
We'll visit the capital, Columbia

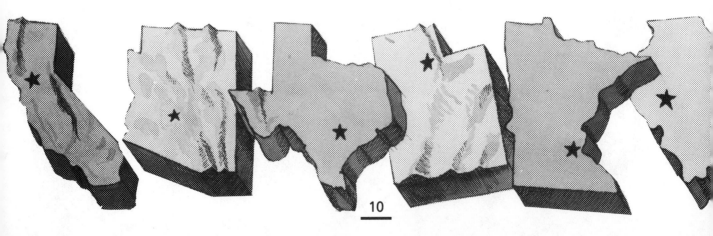

South Dakota has clean crisp air
And its capital city is Pierre
Nashville's the capital of Tennessee
Let's all go to the Jamboree
(Country break)
Austin's the capital of Texas (WHOO!)
Hold on tight when you're riding that
    bronco
Salt Lake City is what we'll call
The capital city of Utah
Montpelier is the capital of Vermont
And you can rap along with us if you want
Virginia was the home to George
    Washington
And its capital city is Richmond
It's pretty easy . . . pretty good
You kind of like it? . . . I knew you would
Olympia's the capital of Washington
Three more (Yeah?) we're almost done
West Virginia, capital . . . Charleston
Learning like this can be a lot of fun
Wisconsin . . . the Dairy State
Madison's the capital . . . can you relate

Wyoming's capital is Cheyenne
You did it . . . now give yourself a hand
    (YAA!)
It's pretty easy . . . pretty good
You kind of like it? . . . I knew you would
Now you've learned the states and
    capitals of our nation
But, there's one more capital that we
    should mention
I bet you've guessed it, because it's so easy
The District of Columbia, or
    Washington, D. C.
It's our nation's capital, where all the
    laws are made
And home to the President of the U.S.A.
Well, have fun learning, and remember
    the rules . . .
Say "NO" to drugs . . . and stay in school
It's pretty easy . . . pretty good
You kind of like it? . . . I knew you would

Source: Rick Kott, "States & Capitals." Utica, MI: Dalka Studios, 1990.

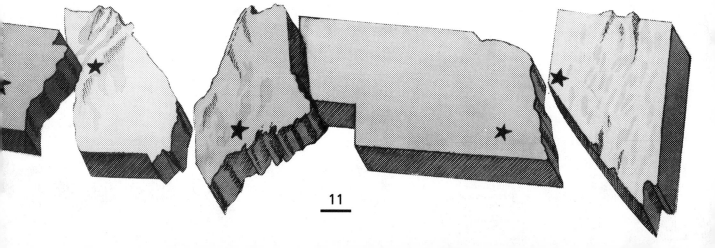

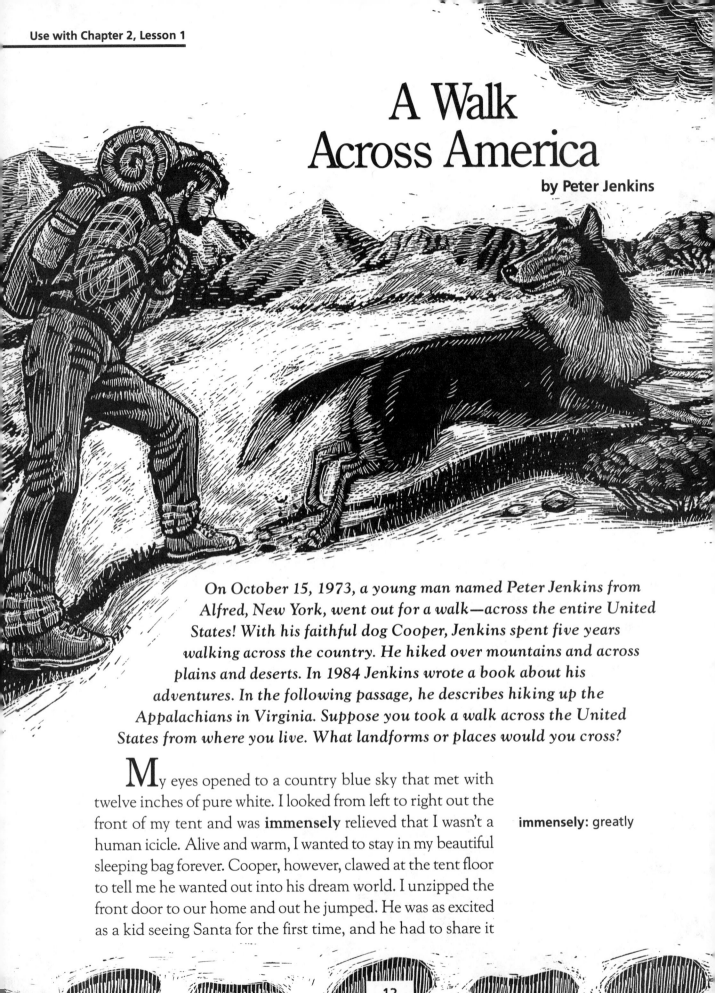

A Walk Across America

by Peter Jenkins

On October 15, 1973, a young man named Peter Jenkins from Alfred, New York, went out for a walk—across the entire United States! With his faithful dog Cooper, Jenkins spent five years walking across the country. He hiked over mountains and across plains and deserts. In 1984 Jenkins wrote a book about his adventures. In the following passage, he describes hiking up the Appalachians in Virginia. Suppose you took a walk across the United States from where you live. What landforms or places would you cross?

My eyes opened to a country blue sky that met with twelve inches of pure white. I looked from left to right out the front of my tent and was **immensely** relieved that I wasn't a human icicle. Alive and warm, I wanted to stay in my beautiful sleeping bag forever. Cooper, however, clawed at the tent floor to tell me he wanted out into his dream world. I unzipped the front door to our home and out he jumped. He was as excited as a kid seeing Santa for the first time, and he had to share it

immensely: greatly

with someone. Of course, that unlucky person was me. After a few minutes of bounding through the **pristine** powder, he crashed into the tent covered with snow and lovingly rolled over on me.

pristine: untouched

Seeing that he was making me fighting mad, he then licked my face with his bad morning breath, strong enough to **singe** my red beard. I tried desperately to crawl deeper into the bag and escape his snowy joy. Too excited to notice, he left the tent. I closed my eyes to get a little more sleep. No sooner had I relaxed when coo-coo Cooper got the cord that held up the front of the tent in his mouth and yanked the tent down with a mighty pull.

singe: burn

Red with rage, I shot out of the sleeping bag far enough to reach outside from under the fallen door into the snow. With both strong hands, I molded a snowball as hard as I could and when teasing Cooper came back to the front, I threw it hard, hoping to hit him in the head. Oh! I was mad! To him that snowball was more fun than baseball so from that day on, Cooper started our winter wake-up, warm-up tradition.

Inching my way far enough out of the cocoonlike bag, I sat up and put on my fluffy down jacket. Then I reached down in the bottom of the six-foot-long sleeping bag and pulled out a variety of crumpled clothes that I left there through the night to keep them warm. My **wadded-up** pants went on, ever so carefully, making sure my body wasn't out of the cozy bag before the warm pants covered the bare spots. With my body all covered, I painfully crawled out of the motherly sleeping blanket and rammed my perfume-producing white socks over my chilly feet. The only thing left to do before we could hit the road was to put on my frosted new boots. The sweat from the day before had **condensed** on the inside of the boots and turned to ice. First my right foot was frozen awake and then my left; it was a battle between the **frigid** frost and the warmth of my feet. My feet won and the stiffened boots stayed on for another traveling day. With that done, I then edged out into the world.

wadded-up: rolled-up

condensed: formed into drops

frigid: freezing

Instead of a steaming cup of coffee, my wake-up **tonic** was taking down the tent. This morning the back end of the tent sagged with six inches of new snow. The front end had already come down with Cooper's pranks, so taking off the rain fly was harder than usual. As I bent slowly to untie the cords from the tent stakes, I heard a fluffy charge from behind. Before I could

tonic: medicine

turn around, Cooper, the muscle-bound elf, was in the air. The next time I saw him he was on top of me. Both of us flattened the once sturdy tent, and there I lay crunched. He was so excited he barked in **hyper** screams. On the rebound, he was off again, darting through the snow as beautifully as a swimming seal.

Again, I reached down into the deep snow and made another snowball. This time I threw it as hard as a pitcher in the World Series and bouncing Cooper caught it in his mouth. Then he trotted over to me and dropped the shattered pieces of the snowball into my hand and ran back into the white field. At about fifty feet he turned around, wagged his tail and barked the way he always did when we used to play throw-the-stick. Shaking my head, I melted. I just couldn't stay mad at this happy dog who only wanted to play. My **irresistible** friend brought, for the thousandth time, a smile like all the sunshine to my face. We played throw-the-snowball-and-run for at least an hour.

The sun was high overhead by the time everything was packed up and ready to go. Back on the road, all I wanted to do was get to North Carolina. It looked only four or five days away, and North Carolina sounded much warmer than West Virginia or Virginia. What slowed us down more than I had expected was all the **continuously** curving roads. On the maps, they looked so straight. Another thing that the maps never told me was that these roads often decided to go up a mountain for four, five, or ten miles at a time. Only a few curves would give some kind of slight relief. For two days crossing through the Jefferson National Forest, we wound our way up and down and up and down through the blowing snow. The farther we went, the more **desolate** and lonely it became. People and stores were almost **extinct**, and it really got bad when we took a left on Highway 16 past Tazewell, Virginia.

We walked over mountains as high as 4,705 feet [1,434 m], weakened by lack of food. It seemed that in this draining cold I could never get enough to eat, even if there had been a store every five miles. We were lucky if we came upon one every fifteen. Then came the mountain that almost made me give up.

We camped early because that mountain stood before us and I knew that this late in the day I shouldn't even try it. I hiked through some bare fields to the top of a wooded hill, set

hyper: excited

irresistible: charming

continuously: without stopping

desolate: empty
extinct: disappeared

up the tent, crawled in, and fell asleep. Cooper was in no mood for play, and he too went to sleep before it was dark.

The morning dawned much too early and we arose in slow motion. Even happy Cooper seemed **lethargic**. He moved at a stumble, like a black bear just waking up from **hibernation**. The whole day was darkened by the gray-black storm clouds blowing in from the west. I took the frosted tent down and we walked down a stubby, cut-over field to the road. There were no houses or stores in sight, so we walked as our shrinking stomachs started burning what little fat we had for fuel. Before us were miles of "Man-eater Mountain." Stubbornly, we started up and went up, and up, and up. Every mile or two I would slow down to a snail's pace because slowing down was the only way I could rest. If I sat down in the warmth-sucking snow, I was afraid I might fall sleep.

lethargic: sleepy

hibernation: a long winter sleep

I fought **depression**. Our enemy became the mountain, and Route 16 became the way to win. Finally I could see it! One mountaintop higher than all the rest and maybe, just maybe, that was the top of Man-eater Mountain. My damp, wrinkled map told me that if I could struggle to the top, I would be able to coast down to the town of Chattam Hill, Virginia, population 58, and please, . . . an **oasis**? I hadn't seen anything human for at least fifteen desolate miles.

depression: sadness

oasis: safe resting spot

I pushed and pushed my aching self and called forth all of my **waning** stores of energy. One hundred feet from me and three hundred from Cooper was the top of Man-eater Mountain. We made it! **Hysterically** I called Cooper.

waning: lessening

hysterically: with a lot of emotion

Screaming, "Cooper! There's the top!" Something in the tone of my holler made Coops run and a few sprinting minutes later we were there. It didn't matter that "there" was in the middle of nowhere: we had made it to the top.

Jenkins made it across the Appalachians. He also made it across the Great Plains and over the Rocky Mountains, finally reaching the Pacific Ocean in 1979—six years after he first set off. In his remarkable journey, Jenkins walked almost 5,000 miles (8,045 km).

Source: Peter Jenkins, *A Walk Across America*. Carmel, NY: Guidepost Publishing Company, 1979.

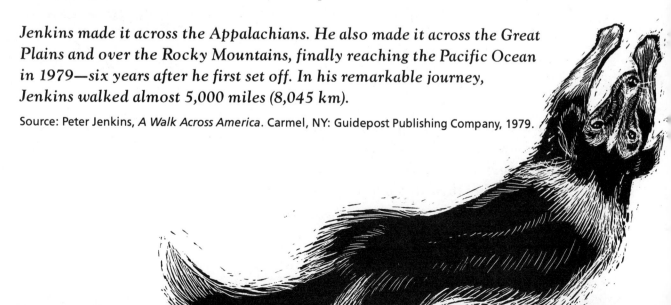

This Is My Rock

by David McCord

When can a rock be a natural resource? Many types of rocks can be used to make buildings, to create energy, and even to make medicine. In the poem below, David McCord describes how a rock is a natural resource for him. He doesn't use the rock as a tool and he doesn't make anything from it. He simply enjoys the beauty of a special place. Do you have a special place where you like to go to enjoy nature?

This is my rock,

And here I run

To steal the secret of the sun;

This is my rock,

And here come I

Before the night has swept the sky;

This is my rock,

This is the place

I meet the evening face to face.

Natural resources are not only valuable because they help industry and agriculture. As David McCord discovered, natural resources are also valuable because they can be enjoyed for their beauty and for the pleasure that people get from seeing them and being around them.

Source: David McCord, *Mr. Bidery's Spidery Garden*. Boston: Little, Brown and Company, 1929.

50 Simple Things Kids Can Do to Save the Earth

by John Javna and the EarthWorks Group

Imagine what your life would be like without your favorite natural resources . . . without a tree to climb, a river to fish in, or a park in which to play. Today's children and adults realize that everyone has to help to protect the environment if we want to enjoy our natural resources in the future. What you may not realize is that you can make a difference! An organization called the EarthWorks Group has printed a book called 50 Simple Things Kids Can Do to Save the Earth. *Here are a few of their suggestions.*

BE A BOTTLE BANDIT

Take a Guess

What is glass made from?

A) Frozen water   B) Sand   C) Venetian blinds

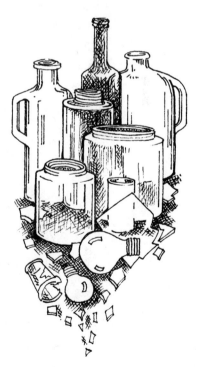

Light bulbs, windows, TVs, mirrors. . . What do they all have in common? Glass.

Look around. See how much glass we use. Now here's an amazing thought: We throw most of our glass away.

Every month, we toss out enough glass bottles and jars to fill up a giant skyscraper.

You probably think this doesn't make much sense, since we're just making more garbage and wasting the Earth's treasures besides. And you're right.

This is especially true because we can reuse them!

Did You Know?

• Glass is **recycled** at factories where they break bottles and jars into little bits, then melt them down and mix them with new glass.

recycled: used again

Answer B. That's right, glass is made from heating and molding sand.

- People have been making glass for over 3,000 years. So when **Nero** was fiddling in ancient Rome, he probably had a bottle of something to drink right next to him.

Nero: an emperor of ancient Rome

- For a long time, glass was considered **precious**. Then people got so good at making it that we started thinking of it as garbage.

precious: very valuable

- Now we throw out 28 billion bottles and jars every year!
- Recycling glass saves energy for making new glass. The energy saved from recycling one glass bottle will light a 100-watt light bulb for four hours.

What You Can Do

To recycle glass bottles and jars in your home:

- Find a place you can keep a box or two for collecting glass.
- If you have enough room, keep a different box for each different color of glass—brown, green, clear. Otherwise, you might have to sort the glass later.
- Take the caps, corks or rings off the bottles and jars. It's okay to leave the paper labels on, but rinse the glass out before you put it in the box.
- Once you've got a place to put the glass, it only takes about 15 minutes a week to keep up the recycling.
- Ask an adult to find out where the nearest recycling center is. Your neighborhood may even have curbside recycling.

STAMP OUT STYROFOAM
Take a Guess

If you lined up all the styrofoam cups made in just one day, how far would they reach?

A) 1 mile   B) Around the earth   C) Across the U.S.

*Y*ou may not know the word "Styrofoam," but you know the stuff. It's a kind of material we use for things like throwaway cups, packing things in boxes, and for keeping "food to go" warm. Lots of fast-food restaurants serve their hamburgers in Styrofoam packages.

Styrofoam is a kind of plastic, so making it uses up treasures that have been on the Earth for billions of years.

Answer: B. Incredible! They would circle the entire planet . . . and reach a little further, too!

And what do we do with it? Go take a look in a fast-food garbage can. Does that **styro-trash** look like the Earth's treasures to you? Not anymore!

Using Styrofoam means using up precious resources... and adding more garbage to our world. Is that what you want? Or do you—and your planet—deserve something better?

Did You Know?

- Styrofoam is permanent garbage. It can't ever become part of the Earth again. Five hundred years from now a [child] might be digging in his [or her] backyard and find a piece of the Styrofoam cup you drank lemonade from on a picnic last week!
- Styrofoam is a danger to sea animals. Floating in the water, it looks like their food. But when they eat it, they're in trouble. Sea turtles, for example, sometimes eat Styrofoam and then—because it makes them float—can't dive again. It eventually clogs their systems, and then they starve to death.

What You Can Do

- Avoid Styrofoam. Such plastic foam is often made with chemicals that make the **ozone** hole bigger!
- If you eat at fast-food restaurants, ask for paper cups and plates. If the people at the restaurant say they don't have them, explain why you don't want to use Styrofoam. Tell them that, as much as you like their food, you really don't want to do anything to hurt the Earth.
- Try to avoid Styrofoam products like picnic plates, cups, and even (if you ever go food shopping) egg cartons.

styro-trash: discarded Styrofoam

ozone: a layer of air high above the earth that protects the planet from harmful rays from the sun

SHOWER POWER
Take a Guess.

How many half-gallon milk cartons can you fill with the water from a five-minute shower?

A) 5   B) 15   C) 50

Answer: C. Think how high 50 milk cartons stacked on top of one another would reach.

19

What if you turned on the faucet and no water came out? We need to save water now so that will never happen!

Did You Know?

- When you shower, you use five gallons of water every minute! How much is that? Enough to fill 40 big glasses!
- A whole shower usually takes at least five minutes. So every day, you could use 25 gallons of water taking one shower.
- In a year, that's almost 10,000 gallons for your showers!
- Taking a bath uses even more water than showers—about twice as much. A bath can easily use 50 gallons of water.
- Shower Secret: People can put in a special "low-flow" shower head. This adds air to the water, so it cuts the amount of shower water used from five gallons a minute to two-and-a-half. That's half as much water! But it feels great!

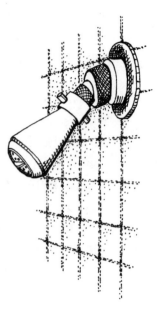

What You Can Do

- Take showers instead of baths. This saves water right away. One bonus: singing in a shower sounds better than in a bath.
- Tell your parents about "low-flow" shower heads. Believe it or not, most grown-ups have never heard of them. You could even phone the hardware store to help find one. Or write a letter to Ecological Water Products, 1341 West Main Rd., Middletown, RI 02840 and ask for information. (If you do this, don't forget to show it to your parents.)

More and more students are getting involved in the fight to clean up pollution and save energy. In the early 1990s, many students decided not to buy food packaged in Styrofoam. Now many fast-food restaurants have stopped using Styrofoam products completely! What other ways can you think of to help protect our environment?

Source: John Javna and the EarthWorks Group, *50 Simple Things Kids Can Do to Save the Earth*. Kansas City: Andrews and McMeel, 1990.

Trash-Busters

from *Kid City News*, 1990

Anne Lindner, Joanna Keiser, and Tiffany McClain were assigned to do a school project for their fifth-grade class in Sorrento Springs, Missouri. They came up with a great idea. It had always bothered them that their school threw away hundreds of plastic lunch trays every day. For their project, they were determined to help put a stop to this waste. Their success brought a lot of attention to them and to their school. The following article from Kid City News is one of many articles that appeared about their project. What does your school do with its cafeteria trays?

Trash Busters

ST. LOUIS, MO – DECEMBER, 1990
Anne Lindner, Joanna Keiser, and Tiffany McClain of Sorrento Springs Elementary School launched a trash attack. These girls discovered that their school district throws out 1,250,000 plastic foam lunch trays in just one year. That's a lot of garbage!

The girls decided to persuade the school district to recycle the trays.

They got eight schools, two fast-food restaurants and several companies in the area to recycle. "The project was great because it was interesting and went so far. And everyone got into it!" said Joanna.

The girls want all the schools and buildings in their district to start recycling in the next year!

Starting a recycling program costs money, so the students convinced companies in the area to help pay for their program. They also convinced the school board to help them with the project. It was hard work, but now their school district recycles more than 1 million trays a year! The governor of Missouri praised the girls at a special ceremony and encouraged other recycling efforts throughout the state.

Source: "Trash-Busters," *Kid City News.* New York: Children's Television Workshop, Dec. 1990.

SYMBOLS OF THE NATION

Why do you think symbols are important? If you live in California or in New York, in Texas or in Minnesota, you may have very different ways of life. But our country's symbols remind us that the 50 states are united as one nation. What does each symbol stand for?

Statue of Liberty

The Statue of Liberty in New York City's harbor has been a symbol of hope and opportunity for the millions of immigrants who saw "Miss Liberty" from their boats as they arrived in the United States. Completed in 1886, it remains a symbol of freedom and liberty for people everywhere.

United States Flag

The 13 stripes represent the 13 original states. The 50 stars represent each state today. As our country has grown, our flag has changed. At least ten different flags have represented our country since the American Revolution. The present flag has been our national symbol since 1960, when Hawaii became the fiftieth state. Every state has its own flag as well. What does your state flag look like?

Liberty Bell

Like the Statue of Liberty, the Liberty Bell is a symbol of freedom. It hung in Independence Hall in Philadelphia where the Declaration of Independence and the United States Constitution were written. It rang on July 4, 1776, to celebrate our first Independence Day.

Great Seal of the United States

Does this seal look familiar? You see it every time you look at a $1 bill. Designed over 200 years ago, the Great Seal of the United States is also found on many documents signed by the President. The American bald eagle is in the center. In one claw is an olive branch, symbolizing peace. In the other are 13 arrows, representing the strength of the 13 original states. The words *E Pluribus Unum* are Latin for "out of many, one." Out of many people, and many states, one united country is formed.

These are just some of the symbols that represent our country and our government. Can you think of any others? Suppose you had to design a symbol for your state. What ideas do you have?

BECOMING A CITIZEN

Today immigrants continue to come to the United States from countries all over the world, seeking to become citizens. Many of these immigrants come with little money, speaking little English. They face the difficult task of filling out forms, waiting in lines, and passing tests — all while adjusting to a new country. To most, it seems like a small price to pay to live in the country of their choice. To make the process of becoming a citizen easier, the United States government has printed a book. This book explains the forms and sample tests that immigrants must fill out. Look at the samples on the next page. What do you think it feels like to be an immigrant hoping to become a United States citizen?

Huma Devi Bairagie is a fourth-grade student from Guyana (gī an′ə), a country in South America. She moved to New York City with her mother and sister in 1991. "I miss my older brother," she says. "But I love the United States. The schools are better and the food is better!" Huma Devi is making new friends. She looks forward to becoming a United States citizen and plans to be a doctor when she grows up.

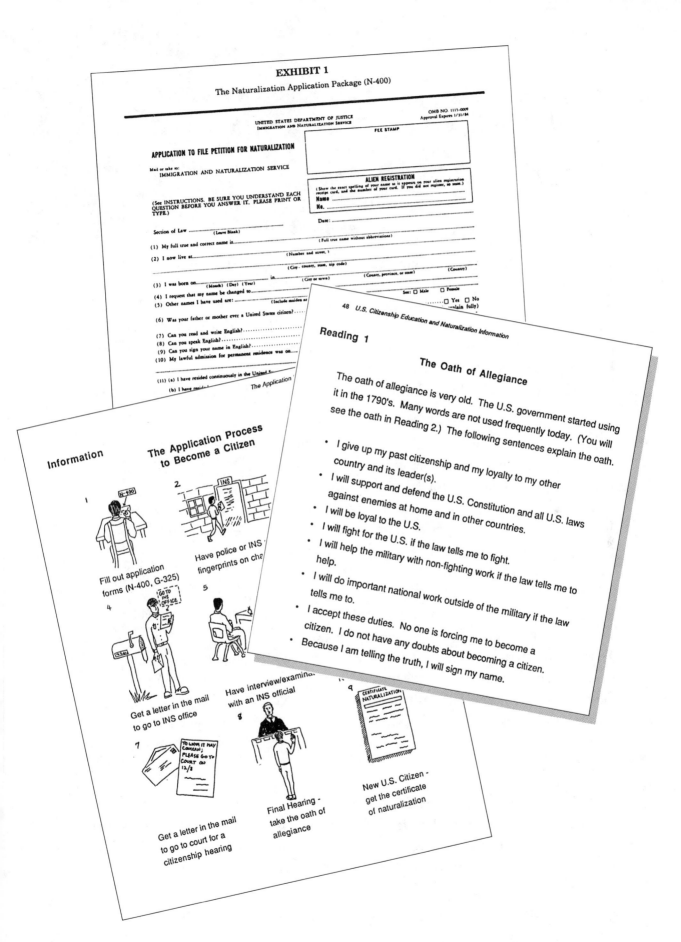

THE NEW COLOSSUS

by Emma Lazarus, 1883

When France gave the United States the Statue of Liberty as a gift in 1880, Emma Lazarus was moved to write the poem, The New Colossus. A colossus is something gigantic. Emma Lazarus was born in New York City in 1849. As a young woman, she saw both her city and the United States change with the constant flow of immigrants from other countries. Many arrived penniless, carrying just a bundle of clothing. But they also came with great dreams of starting a new life in a new land. Who is the Statue of Liberty welcoming?

Not like the **brazen** giant of Greek fame,
With **conquering** limbs **astride** from land to land;
Here at our sea-washed, sunset gates shall stand
A mighty woman with a torch, whose flame
Is the **imprisoned** lightning, and her name
Mother of **Exiles**. From her **beacon-hand**
Glows world-wide welcome; her mild eyes command
The air-bridged harbor that twin cities frame.

"Keep, ancient lands, your **storied pomp!**" cries she
With silent lips. "Give me your tired, your poor,
Your **huddled masses** yearning to breathe free,
The **wretched refuse** of your **teeming** shore.
Send these, the homeless, **tempest-tost** to me,
I lift my lamp beside the golden door!"

brazen: bold
conquering: mighty
astride: with one leg on each side

imprisoned: captured
exiles: people forced out of their countries
beacon-hand: hand that holds a guiding light

storied pomp: old habits and fancy ways
huddled masses: crowds of poor people
wretched refuse: unwanted people
teeming: crowded
tempest-tost: battered by storms

The New Colossus was carved into a bronze plaque and mounted at the base of the Statue of Liberty when the statue was completed in 1886. Today, the statue still welcomes people coming to the United States through New York Harbor. The statue symbolizes hope and freedom to millions of people throughout the world.

Source: Emma Lazarus, *Poems of Emma Lazarus.* Boston: Houghton-Mifflin Company, 1889.

THE NORTHEAST

There is a time between the seasons. It comes in March when winter seems tired and spring is only a hoped-for thing.

from *Sugaring Time*
by Kathryn Lasky

THE WALUM OLUM

by the Lenape-Algonquian People, 1700s

Almost every group of people has a story about how the world began and how their people came to live in it. The Walum Olum is a story told by the Lenape Algonquian people, an Indian group who were living in what is today Pennsylvania, New Jersey, and Delaware long before Europeans arrived. They handed this story down from generation to generation for hundreds of years. Then some time in the 1700s they wrote the Walum Olum in pictographs—drawings made of symbols that tell a story. Look at this selection from the Walum Olum below. Which pictographs can you understand without reading the words beside them? According to the Walum Olum, what is the explanation of the beginning of the world?

 1. At first, in that place, at all times, above the earth,

 2. On the earth, an extended fog, and there the **great Manito** was.

great Manito: great Spirit

 3. At first, forever, lost in space, everywhere, the great Manito was.

 4. He made the extended land and the sky.

 5. He made the sun, the moon, the stars.

 6. He made them all to move evenly.

 7. Then the wind blew violently, and it cleared, and the water flowed off far and strong.

 8. And groups of islands grew newly, and there remained.

 9. **Anew** spoke the great Manito, a manito to manitos,

anew: again

 10. To **beings, mortals,** souls and all,

beings, mortals: people

 11. And ever after he was a manito to men, and their grandfather.

28

12. He gave the first mother, the mother of beings.

 13. He gave the fish, he gave the turtles, he gave the beasts, he gave the birds.

 14. But an evil Manito made evil beings only, monsters.

 15. He made the flies, he made the gnats.

 16. All beings were then friendly.

 17. Truly the manitos were active and kindly

 18. To those very first men, and to those first mothers; fetched them wives,

 19. And fetched them food, when first they desired it.

 20. All had cheerful knowledge, all had leisure, all thought in gladness.

 21. But very secretly an evil being, a mighty magician, came on earth,

 22. And with him brought badness, quarreling, unhappiness.

 23. Brought bad weather, brought sickness, brought death.

 24. All this took place **of old** on the earth, beyond the great tide water, at the first.   **of old:** a long time ago

The pictograph language helped to keep the story of the Walum Olum alive. Think of a story or something you believe in. How might you use pictographs to share your ideas with someone else?

Source: Daniel Garrison Brinton, *The Lenape and Their Legends*. Philadelphia: Library of Aboriginal American Literature, 1884.

Sugaring Time

by Kathryn Lasky

Have you ever had maple syrup on your pancakes for breakfast? Where do you think the syrup comes from? In Sugaring Time you will read the true story of the Lacey family. They make maple syrup on their tree farm in Vermont. The Laceys gather maple sap every year the way that New England farmers have been gathering it for hundreds of years. As you read this selection, see if you can explain what the Lacey children like best about "sugaring time."

There is a time between the seasons. It comes in March when winter seems tired and spring is only a hoped-for thing. The **crystalline** whiteness of February has **vanished** and there is not yet even the pale green stain in the trees that promises spring. It is a time out of time, when night, in central Vermont, can bring a **fitful** late winter storm that eases, the very next day, into sunshine and a melting wind from the southeast.

Many people complain about this time of year. Snow cannot be counted on for sledding or skiing; cars get stuck in muddy roads; clothes are mud-caked and hard to clean; and the old folks' **arthritis** kicks up. Everyone, young and old, gets cranky about staying indoors.

But for a few people, this time is a season in its own right. For them it is sugaring time, when the sap begins to flow in the maple grove or **sugarbush**, as it is called. It is a time that **contradicts** all farming calendars that say crops are planted in the spring, cared for in the summer, and harvested in the fall. This crop, maple sap, is harvested in March, and that is part of the specialness of sugaring time. It is special, too, because young people have a reason to go outside, snow or no snow,

crystalline: pure
vanished: disappeared

fitful: stormy

arthritis: a disease causing pain in one's joints

sugarbush: group of maple trees where sap is gathered
contradicts: goes against

mud or no mud, and older people have a reason to believe in the coming spring.

Alice and Don Lacey and their three children live on a farm that has a small sugarbush. They have been waiting almost two weeks for the sap to start running. . . .

Tapping Time

The big trails have been **broken out**. Another cold spell comes, giving the Laceys just enough time to get the tapholes drilled into the maple trees and the buckets hung before the sap starts rising again.

They load up the sled with buckets and lids, called hats, and spouts. In all, nearly two hundred holes will be drilled, two hundred spouts hammered into the holes, and two hundred buckets hung. Alice fetches the drill and bit. . . .

The runners glide over the freshly broken trails. It is a cold, windless day. The sky is clear, and in the deep silence of the woods one bird can be heard singing. The trees stand waiting, ready to give up some of the clear sap that circulates just beneath the bark. Alice and Don will drill carefully. Often, more than one hole is drilled in a tree, especially if it is a good running tree. But they will not go too deep or drill too many holes at a time in one tree. They mean to take only a little of each tree's sap, for that is its source of **vitality**, its **nourishment**, its life. . . .

Alice and Don begin to drill. The bit, or pointed part of the drill, is just under one-half inch in **diameter** and the holes are no more than one and one-half inches deep. The holes are slanted upward into the tree to catch the sap, for although the saying is "Sap's rising!" the movement of the sap within the tree is downward as well as upward, around about, and every which way. . . .

"Sap's Rising!"

The frost designs on Jonathan's bedroom window have melted before he has dressed this morning. Bright **lances** of sunlight do a crazy crisscross dance on Angie's covers if she wiggles her knees. Little Jeremy climbs up on a stool by his window and takes a quiet look at the sunlit world outside.

"Sap's rising!" Alice calls up. "It's going to flow today!". . . .

The sap flows all day, not in little drips or plinks, but in

broken out: blazed; snow-plowed

vitality: life and health

nourishment: food

diameter: distance across a round object

lances: darts

what Jonathan calls long "drrriiips." It is the sweet maple song of spring to Jonathan's and Angie's ears as they stand in the sugarbush. By tomorrow, they tell each other, the buckets will be full enough to gather. Angie and Jonathan lift the hats and peek into the buckets. The sparkling sap, clear and bright, runs like streams of Christmas tinsel. They each take a lick and wonder how so much **crystal** sweetness can come from a **gnarled** tree older than all their grandparents put together.

crystal: clear
gnarled: twisted

They stop at the first stand of maples. Jonathan removes a hat from a bucket. It is brim-full, and a world is mirrored in its crystalline surface. Bark **shimmers**, branches **quiver**, a whole sky with clouds and sunbursts is reflected in the tree's sweet water. It is a bucketful of life that Jonathan cannot resist. He dips a jar into the sap for the first real taste of spring, and then begins gathering. He and Angie and their father pour the contents of the tree buckets into the gathering bucket. This special container has a **flared** rim, so the sap will not slosh over as it is carried to the gathering tank on the sled. It is heavy work. One full gathering bucket can weigh nearly thirty pounds. . . .

shimmers: shines
quiver: shake

flared: widened

Boiling

The trees have nearly finished their run. The sap has all been gathered and waits in the storage tank behind the sugarhouse. It must be boiled within a week or it may spoil. Forty gallons of sap will become only one gallon of syrup, so it is **inefficient** to boil small quantities. Now that the tank is full, boiling can begin.

One morning, the melting, earthy smell of spring up in the meadow suddenly turns sweet a few hundred feet from the sugarhouse. Steam rolls out the open ends of the house and smoke rises from the chimney in back. Being inside is like sitting in a maple cloud surrounded by the muffled roar of the fire and the bubbling tumble of boiling sap. Betty Brown and the children are there, their cheeks wet and shiny in the mapley mist. This is their first celebration, except birthdays, since Christmas. Boiling time is like a party, a party that celebrates mud and greenness, sweetness and renewed life.

inefficient: a waste of time

The Sweet Taste

On a windless, starry night, it started again, coming down softly, almost secretly, and covering everything with its sparkling whiteness on Easter eve. It is an April snowfall, the very last snowfall of the season. The children are thrilled, for it means a sugar-on-snow party with the new maple syrup. The cold sweet taste is much better than jelly beans or even chocolate Easter eggs. Alice boils the syrup until it is foamy and slightly thicker. Then the children race with the pan of warm syrup to the meadow's corner, followed by Alice, carrying cider and doughnuts. They smooth and pack a place in the small patch of snow and pour the syrup, sometimes dribbling it in designs that look like twisting rivers or sometimes pooling it into golden puddles.

Within a few seconds it grows cold and waxy and chewy. They twist it around forks or pick it up with their fingers and eat it. They drink the last of the year's cider with the first of the year's syrup and eat powdered doughnuts. This is the second taste of the new maple syrup. The first was a pancake breakfast, the morning after the boiling. . . .

Within four weeks it is all over. The shortest season of all is finished. The sap has stopped running, but its sweet syrup will be tasted throughout the rest of the year: There will be pancake breakfasts almost weekly, maple candy for trick or treat at Halloween, gifts at Christmas, and more sugar-on-snow parties in the winter to come, when the whole meadow lies under a blanket of snow for months and months.

Sugaring time ends in April, and for the rest of the year the maple trees will make and store sap deep inside their roots and in their trunks. Winter is long and cold in the northeastern region of the United States, but late winter brings a special time—sugaring time—that the Laceys and other maple farmers look forward to. The next time you pour maple syrup on your pancakes, think how much work—and fun—went into making your breakfast sweeter!

Source: Kathryn Lasky, *Sugaring Time.* New York: Macmillan Publishing Company, 1983.

THE LUMBERMAN'S ALPHABET

Traditional Loggers' Song

The forests of the United States once stretched from the Northeast across to the Middle West and all the way up into Canada. In the 1800s companies hired groups of workers to spend the winter deep in the forests, cutting trees down for lumber. These lumberjacks, or shanty boys as they sometimes called themselves, lived together in camps all winter while they worked in the cold forests. In the evenings, they sat around together and made up songs like this one. How do the words give an idea of a lumberjack's daily life? If you were to write a song about your life—"The Student's Alphabet"—what would your letters stand for?

Not too fast

1. A is for Ax, and that we all know, And B is for

Boy that can use it al - so; C is for Chop-ping we

first do be - gin, And D is for Dan-ger we oft - en fall in.

So mer - ry, _____ so mer - ry are we, No

mor - tals on earth are as hap - py as we. T' me

I der - ry O der - ry I der - ry down, Use
shan - ty boys well and there's noth - ing goes wrong.

2. E is for Echo that through the woods rang,
   And F is for Foreman, the head of our gang;
   G is for Grindstone at night we do turn,
   And H is for Handle so smoothly worn.

3. I is for Iron which we mark our pine,
   And J is for Jovial we're always incline';
   K is for Keen Edge our axes we keep,
   And L is for Lice that keep us from sleep.

4. M is for Moss which we chink our camp,
   And N is for Needle with which we mend
     our pants;
   O is for Owl which hooted at night,
   And P is for Pine which we always fall right.

5. Q is for Quickness we put ourselves to,
   R is for River we haul the logs to;
   S is for Sleds we haul the logs on,
   T is for Team that pulls them along.

6. U is for Uses we put ourselves to,
   And V is for Valley we haul the logs
     through;
   And W is for Woods we leave in the spring,
   And I have not sung all I'm goin' to sing.

7. X is for Christmas when the yarding's all
     done,
   Y is for Yonder, the set of the sun;
   Zed is for Zero, in the cold winter time,
   And now I have brought all these letters
     in rhyme.

Source: William Main Doerflinger, *Songs of the Sailor and Lumberman.* New York: The Macmillan Company, 1972.

HARD TIMES AT VALLEY FORGE

by Joseph Martin, 1777–1778

Supplies often ran low during the American Revolution. When General George Washington's army marched to Valley Forge, Pennsylvania, in December 1777, soldiers had little food, clothing, or medicine. One of these soldiers was Joseph Martin, a 17-year-old boy from Milford, Connecticut. Martin kept a diary of those hard times. How do you think people stand such hardships?

The army was now not only starved but naked. **The greatest part** were not only shirtless and barefoot, but **destitute of** all other clothing, especially blankets. I **procured** a small piece of raw cowhide and made myself a pair of moccasins, which kept my feet (while they lasted) from the frozen ground, although, as I well remember, the hard edges so **galled** my ankles, while on a march, that it was with much difficulty and pain that I could wear them afterwards; but the only **alternative** I had was to **endure** this inconvenience or to go barefoot, as hundreds of my companions had to, till they might be tracked by their blood upon the rough frozen ground. But hunger, nakedness and sore shins were not the only difficulties we had at that time to **encounter**; we had hard duty to perform and little or no strength to perform it with.

The army . . . marched for the Valley Forge in order to take up our winter **quarters**. We were now in a truly **forlorn** condition,—no clothing, no **provisions** and as disheartened as need be. . . . Our **prospect** was indeed **dreary**. In our miserable condition, to go into the wild woods and build us **habitations**

greatest part: most
destitute of: lacking
procured: got

galled: scraped

alternative: choice
endure: put up with

encounter: deal with
quarters: housing
forlorn: sad
provisions: goods, especially food
prospect: situation
dreary: gloomy
habitations: places to live

...in such a weak, starved and naked condition, was appalling in the highest degree. ... However, there was no **remedy**, no alternative but this or **dispersion**. But dispersion, I believe, was not thought of, at least, I did not think of it. We had engaged in the defense of our injured country and were willing, nay, we were determined to **persevere** as long as such hardships were not altogether **intolerable**. ...

remedy: cure
dispersion: breaking up of the army

persevere: continue
intolerable: unbearable

We arrived at the Valley Forge in the evening [December 18]. It was dark; there was no water to be found and I was **perishing with** thirst. I searched for water till I was weary and came to my tent without finding any. Fatigue and thirst, joined with hunger, almost made me desperate. I felt at that instant as if I would have taken **victuals** or drink from the best friend I had on earth by force. I am not writing fiction, all are **sober realities**. Just after I arrived at my tent, two soldiers, whom I did not know, passed by. They had some water in their canteens which they told me they had found a good distance off, but could not direct me to the place as it was very dark. I tried to beg a **draught** of water from them but they . . . [refused]. At length I persuaded them to sell me a drink for three **pence**, Pennsylvania currency, which was every cent of property I could then call my own, so great was the necessity I was then reduced to.

perishing with: dying of

victuals: food
sober realities: hard truths

draught [draft]: drink
pence: pennies

I lay here two nights and one day and had not a **morsel** of anything to eat all the time, **save** half of a small pumpkin, which I cooked by placing it upon a rock, the skin side uppermost, and making a fire upon it. By the time it was heat[ed] through I devoured it with as keen an appetite as I should a pie made of it at some other time.

morsel: scrap
save: except for

Nearly 3,000 soldiers died at Valley Forge during the winter of 1777-1778—roughly 30 soldiers a day. If the British had attacked they probably could have won an easy victory over the sick and starving American army. But the British never tried. In February 1778, Baron von Steuben, a German officer, came to Valley Forge and helped train and reorganize the troops. Soon American soldiers were healthy and ready for battle. Joseph Martin grew healthier, too, and served in the army until the war's final day. He then became a schoolteacher and laborer and settled in Prospect, Maine.

Source: Joseph Martin, *A Narrative of Some of the Adventures, Dangers and Sufferings of a Revolutionary Soldier.* Hallowell, Maine, 1830; reprinted Boston: Little, Brown & Company, 1962.

Yaacov's Journey

by Evelyn Wilde Mayerson

In 1910 almost 1 million immigrants arrived in the United States. Many of these immigrants passed through Ellis Island, near the Statue of Liberty in New York City. If an immigrant had a serious problem—such as a disease or a physical handicap—an inspector could force the immigrant to return to his or her native land. In the following story, a nine-year-old boy named Yaacov (yä′ kəf) has just arrived with his family at Ellis Island in 1910. Yaacov is deaf and cannot speak. His family fears that the inspectors will send him back to Poland. While the story is fiction, it is based on a true tale told by a grandmother to her granddaughter. The granddaughter, Evelyn Wilde Mayerson, wrote this tale in 1990. How do you think Yaacov felt during the interview with the inspector?

Yaacov stood before the high bench in his **knickers** and **visored** hat. When the inspector asked him his name, his mother Raizel stepped forward. "He has a sore throat," she explained. "Not a sickness. Just hoarse. From calling geese. See, I have wrapped his neck in flannel."

"You've been on the ship for two weeks," said the inspector when the interpreter had relayed Raizel's answer. "As far as I know, there was not a goose among you." He laughed at his own joke.

Then things took a serious turn. The officials **conferred**. One stepped behind Yaacov and clapped his hands behind Yaacov's head. Chanah, who saw this coming, pointed from the fence and Yaacov turned.

"He seems to hear all right," said the interpreter.

"I'm not so sure," said the inspector. "He was slow in turning. Whisper your name, boy. Even with a sore throat, you can whisper."

knickers: short pants
visored: with a brim

conferred: spoke together

"He wants your name," said the interpreter.

Yaacov drew an imaginary line down the center of his body, turned in one direction, then the other. Then he fell to the ground, rolling and **thrashing** on the floor.

"What is he doing?" asked the inspector. "Is he having some kind of fit? If that's what he's doing, the interview is over."

Chanah broke from her family, ducked beneath the iron pipe, and ran to the high bench. "I know what he's doing. He's showing you Yaacov, in the Bible. That's his name. That's what he's saying."

"Yaacov is Jacob," explained the interpreter. The inspector leaned over his desk to peer at Chanah. "Who are you to him?" he asked.

"He's my cousin."

"How do you know that was what he said?"

"Yaacov in the Bible was a twin. That's why he divided himself in half. And when he fell to the ground, that was Yaacov wrestling with the Angel. He can talk," insisted Chanah. "He just talks with his hands. Tell him something else," she said to Yaacov.

Yaacov pointed to the inspector's pocket watch, made **rippling** hand motions, then a pinch of his thumb and **forefinger**.

"He's saying you have a drop of water inside your watchcase."

The inspector looked. Sure enough, there was a tiny drop of water under the case.

"At least we know his eyesight is good," he said.

The inspector appeared to be troubled. He seemed to be thinking, you let in someone who's deaf, then you let in someone else who's blind. Where's it all going to end?

When the inspector shook his head, nobody needed an interpreter to figure out that Yaacov would not be permitted to enter.

A great scream went up from Raizel, the kind that rattles from the throat and makes those hearing feel their scalps crawl.

The interpreter, used to such scenes, explained, "The boy has to return. The mother and the other boy can stay, but this one has to return to Poland."

Raizel began to shriek and tear at her hair while every other mother and father in the room pressed forward with their

their hands at their hearts, their throats, knowing that at any time this could happen to them.

Yaacov's mother was in a painful **dilemma**. What to do? Her choice was simple, yet terrible. To return with Yaacov, and perhaps never see her husband, Shimson, again; worse, to let Yaacov return alone to live with distant relatives, perhaps never to see him again.

dilemma: difficult situation

Chanah approached the inspector's bench. "He knows everything," she said. "He can tell you what you had for breakfast this morning and what you had for lunch."

"All right," the inspector said. "Tell him to tell me what I had to eat today."

Chanah asked Yaacov. Yaacov in turn made hand motions that Chanah interpreted.

"He said you had sausage and bread for lunch with coffee to drink, and eggs for breakfast."

"I'll be," said the inspector. "How did he do that?"

Chanah conferred with Yaacov. "He smells the sausage on your breath, and he sees the coffee on your teeth, the bread crumbs on your beard, and the eggs on your mustache."

The inspector cocked an eye. "How does he know that I didn't have the eggs for lunch?"

"Because the egg on your mustache is dry. If you had had it for lunch, the pieces would still be damp."

The two men looked at each other while everyone held their breath. Then the inspector winked at the interpreter. "I say we let in a kid with a sore throat." No translation was needed. The smiles told it all.

When the inspector stamped a landing permit for Yaacov, Yaacov's mother grabbed his hand and kissed it.

"Oh now," said the inspector, "don't be making me out to be some saint." Then he became all business. "Next," he shouted, "we haven't got all day," as another family with patient, hopeful eyes came forward, bringing their belongings on their backs and their children in their arms.

Yaacov's quick thinking and intelligence helped convince the inspector to let him into the United States. Not all immigrants were as lucky as Yaacov. That same year, over 20,000 people were turned back from Ellis Island and forced to return to the countries from which they had come.

Source: Evelyn Wilde Mayerson, *The Cat Who Escaped from Steerage.* New York: Macmillan Publishing Company, 1990.

In the Year of the Boar and Jackie Robinson

by Bette Bao Lord

Coming to the United States as an immigrant can be a puzzling experience, especially if you are a child. Even saying the Pledge of Allegiance or playing an American game can be confusing for a new immigrant. In Bette Bao Lord's novel, Shirley Temple Wong and her mother come to the United States from China in 1947. Shirley finds herself in a fifth-grade classroom in Brooklyn in New York City, struggling to make sense of baseball, the English language, and American customs. Bette Bao Lord's novel is fiction, but the author was herself an immigrant from China and experienced many of the difficulties that immigrants face when they have to get used to a new culture. According to Shirley's teacher, in what ways is Shirley like the baseball hero Jackie Robinson?

It was almost summer. An eager sun outshone the neon sign atop the Squibb factory even before the first bell **beckoned** students to their homerooms. Now alongside the empty milk crates at Mr. P's, brown paper bags with collars neatly rolled boasted plump strawberries, **crimson** cherries and Chiquita bananas. The cloakroom stood empty. Gone, the sweaters, **slickers** and **galoshes**.

At the second bell, the fifth grade, as always, scrambled to their feet. As always, Tommy O'Brien giggled, and each girl checked her seat to see if she was his victim of the day. Susie Spencer, whose tardiness could set clocks, rushed in, her face long with excuses. Popping a last bubble, Maria Gonzales tucked her gum safely behind an ear while Joseph gave an extra stroke to his hair.

beckoned: called

crimson: red

slickers: plastic raincoats
galoshes: rain boots

41

Finally Mrs. Rappaport cleared her throat, and the room was still. With hands over hearts, the class performed the ritual that ushered in another day at school.

Shirley's voice was lost in the chorus.

"I pledge a lesson to the frog of the United States of America, and to the wee puppet for witches' hands. One Asian, in the vestibule, with little tea and just rice for all."

"Class, be seated," said Mrs. Rappaport, looking around to see if anyone was absent.

No one was.

"Any questions on the homework?"

All hands remained on or below the decks, etched with initials, new with splinters, brown with age.

"In that case, any questions on any subject at all?"

Irvie's hand shot up. It was quickly pulled down by Maria, who hated even the sound of the word "spider." Spiders were all Irvie ever asked about, talked about, dreamed about. How many eyes do spiders have? Do spiders eat three meals a day? Where are spiders' ears located?

By now, everyone in the fifth grade knew that spiders come with no, six or eight eyes. That spiders do not have to dine regularly and that some can thrive as long as two years without a bite. That spiders are earless.

Since Irvie was as scared of girls as Maria was of spiders, he sat on his hands, but just in case he changed his mind, Maria's hand went up.

"Yes, Maria?"

"Eh . . . eh, I had a question, but I forgot."

"Was it something we discussed yesterday?"

"Yeah, yeah, that's it."

"Something about air currents or cloud formation, perhaps?"

"Yeah. How come I see lightning before I hear thunder?"

"Does anyone recall the answer?"

Tommy jumped in. "That's easy. 'Cause your eyes are in front, and your ears are off to the side." To prove his point, he wiggled his ears, which framed his **disarming** smile like the handles of a fancy soup bowl.

disarming: charming

Laughter was his reward.

"The correct answer, Maria," said Mrs. Rappaport, trying not to smile too, "is that light waves travel faster than sound waves."

Shirley raised her hand.

"Yes?"

"Who's the girl Jackie Robinson?"

Laughter returned. This time Shirley did not understand the joke. Was the girl very, very bad? So bad that her name should not be uttered in the presence of a grown-up?

Putting a finger to her lips, Mrs. Rappaport quieted the class. "Shirley, you ask an excellent question. A most **appropriate** one...."

appropriate: fitting

The Chinese blushed, wishing her teacher would stop praising her, or at least not in front of the others. Already, they called her "teacher's dog" or "apple shiner."

"Jackie Robinson," Mrs. Rappaport continued, "is a man, the first Negro to play baseball in the major leagues."

"What is a Negro, Mrs. Rappaport?"

"A Negro is someone who is born with dark skin."

"Like Mabel?"

"Like Mabel and Joey and . . . "

"Maria?"

"No, Maria is not a Negro."

"But Maria is dark. Darker than Joey."

"I see what you mean. Let me try again. A Negro is someone whose **ancestors** originally came from Africa and who has dark skin."

ancestors: relatives from long ago

"Then why I'm called Jackie Robinson?"

Mrs. Rappaport looked mystified. "Who calls you Jackie Robinson?"

"Everybody."

"Then I'll have to ask them. Mabel?"

" 'Cause she's **pigeon-toed** and stole home."

pigeon-toed: a person whose feet point toward each other

The teacher nodded. "Well, Shirley, it seems you are not only a good student, but a good baseball player."

There, she'd done it again! The kids would surely call her "a shiner of apples for teacher's dog" next. Shirley's unhappiness must have been obvious, because Mrs. Rappaport evidently felt the need to explain further.

"It is a compliment, Shirley. Jackie Robinson is a big hero, especially in Brooklyn, because he plays for the Dodgers."

"Who is dodgers?" Shirley asked.

That question, like a **wayward** torch in a roomful of firecrackers, sparked answers from everyone.

wayward: stray

"De Bums!"

"The best in the history of baseball!"

"Kings of Ebbets Field!"

"They'll kill the Giants!"

"They'll murder the Yankees!"

"The swellest guys in the world!"

"America's favorites!"

"Winners!"

Mrs. Rappaport clapped her hands for order. The girls quieted down first, followed **reluctantly** by the boys. That's better. Participation is welcome, but one at a time. Let's do talk about baseball!"

reluctantly: without wanting to

"Yay!" shouted the class.

"And let's combine it with **civics** too!"

civics: citizenship

The class did not welcome this proposal as eagerly, but Mrs. Rappaport went ahead anyway.

"Mabel, tell us why baseball is America's favorite **pastime**."

Pursing her lips in disgust at so ridiculous a question, Mabel answered. " 'Cause it's a great game. Everybody plays it, loves it and follows the games on the radio and **nabs** every chance to go and see it."

"True," said Mrs. Rappaport, nodding. "But what is it about baseball that is ideally suited to Americans?"

Mabel turned around, looking for an answer from someone else, but **to no avail**. There was nothing to do but throw the question back. "Whatta ya mean by 'suits'?"

"I mean, is there something special about baseball that fits the special kind of people we are and the special kind of country America is?" Mrs. Rappaport tilted her head to one side, inviting a response. When none came, she sighed a sigh so **fraught with** disappointment that it sounded as if her heart were breaking.

No one wished to be a party to such a sad event, so everybody found some urgent business to attend to like scratching, slumping, sniffing, scribbling, squinting, sucking teeth or removing dirt from underneath a fingernail. Joseph cracked his knuckles.

The ticking of the big clock became so loud that President Washington and President Lincoln, who occupied the wall space to either side of it, exchanged a look of shared displeasure.

But within the frail, birdlike body of Mrs. Rappaport was the spirit of a dragon capable of tackling the heavens and earth. With a quick toss of her red hair, she proceeded to answer her own question with such feeling that no one who heard could be so unkind as to ever forget. Least of all Shirley.

"Baseball is not just another sport. America is not just another country. . . . "

If Shirley did not understand every word, she took its meaning to heart. Unlike Grandfather's stories which quieted the warring spirits within her with the softness of moonlight or the **lyric timbre** of a lone flute, Mrs. Rappaport's speech thrilled her like sunlight and trumpets.

"In our national pastime, each player is a member of a team, but when he comes to bat, he stands alone. One man. Many opportunities. For no matter how far behind, how late in the game, he, by himself, can make a difference. He can change what has been. He can make it a new ball game.

pastime: hobby

nabs: grabs

to no avail: with no luck

fraught with: full of

lyric timbre: tone

45

"In the life of our nation, each man is a citizen of the United States, but he has the right to pursue his own happiness. For no matter what his race, religion or creed, be he **pauper** or president, he has the right to speak his mind, to live as he wishes within the law, to elect our officials and stand for office, to **excel**. To make a difference. To change what has been. To make a better America.

"And so can you! And so must you!"

Shirley felt as if the walls of the classroom had vanished. **In their stead** was a frontier of doors to which she held the keys.

"This year, Jackie Robinson is at bat. He stands for himself, for Americans of every **hue**, for an America that honors fair play.

"Jackie Robinson is the grandson of a slave, the son of a **sharecropper**, raised in poverty by a lone mother who took in ironing and washing. But a woman determined to achieve a better life for her son. And she did. For despite **hostility** and **injustice**, Jackie Robinson went to college, excelled in all sports, served his country in war. And now, Jackie Robinson is at bat in the big leagues. Jackie Robinson is making a difference. Jackie Robinson has changed what has been. And Jackie Robinson is making a better America.

"And so can you! And so must you!"

Suddenly Shirley understood why her father had brought her ten thousand miles to live among strangers. Here, she did not have to wait for gray hairs to be considered wise. Here, she could speak up, question even the conduct of the President. Here, Shirley Temple Wong was somebody. She felt as if she had the power of ten tigers, as if she had grown as tall as the Statue of Liberty.

pauper: poor person

excel: do very well

in their stead: instead

hue: color

sharecropper: a farmer who rents land by paying a share of the crop raised on the land

hostility: anger

injustice: unfair ways

Shirley learns to speak English fluently and makes friends with her American classmates. They are all delighted when Jackie Robinson wins the "Rookie of the Year" award and the Dodgers win the National League pennant. You can read the novel to find out how Shirley actually meets her hero, Jackie Robinson.

Source: Bette Bao Lord, *In the Year of the Boar and Jackie Robinson*. New York: Harper & Row, 1984.

The Cricket in Times Square

by George Selden

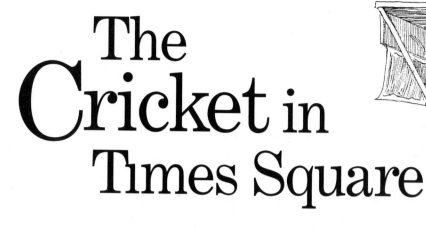

New York City is the largest city in the United States. It is not a place where a person finds many wild animals—especially ones that chirp! In George Selden's novel, a boy named Mario Bellini works at his parents' newsstand at the subway station underneath Times Square. One day Mario hears something chirping near the newsstand. What does the selection teach about city life?

Mario heard the sound too. He stood up and listened intently. The noise of the **shuttle** rattled off into silence. From the streets above came the quiet murmur of the late traffic. There was a noise of rustling nothingness in the station. Still Mario listened, straining to catch the mysterious sound. . . . And there it came again.

shuttle: a subway in New York City

It was like a quick stroke across the strings of a violin, or like a harp that had been plucked suddenly. If a leaf in a green forest far from New York had fallen at midnight through the darkness into a **thicket**, it might have sounded like that.

thicket: a thick group of bushes

Mario thought he knew what it was. The summer before he had gone to visit a friend who lived on Long Island. One afternoon, as the low sun reached long yellow fingers through the tall grass, he had stopped beside a meadow to listen to just such a noise. But there had been many of them then—a chorus. Now there was only one. Faintly it came again through the subway station.

Mario slipped out of the newsstand and stood waiting. The next time he heard the sound, he went toward it. It seemed to come from one corner, next to the stairs that led up to Forty-second Street. Softly Mario went toward the spot. For several minutes there was only the whispering silence. Whatever it was that was making the sound had heard him coming and was quiet. Silently Mario waited. Then he heard it again, rising from a pile of waste papers and **soot** that had blown against the concrete wall.

soot: ashes

He went down and very gently began to lift off the papers. One by one he **inspected** them and laid them to one side. Down near the bottom the papers became dirtier and dirtier. Mario reached the floor. He began to feel with his hands through the dust and soot. And wedged in a crack under all the **refuse**, he found what he'd been looking for.

inspected: looked at closely

refuse: garbage

It was a little insect, about an inch long and covered with dirt. It had six legs, two long antennae on its head and what seemed to be a pair of wings folded on its back. Holding his discovery as carefully as his fingers could, Mario lifted the insect up and rested him in the palm of his hand.

"A cricket!" he exclaimed.

Keeping his cupped hand very steady, Mario walked back to the newsstand. The cricket didn't move. And he didn't make that little musical noise any more. He just lay perfectly still— as if he were sleeping, or frightened to death.

Mario pulled out a tissue of Kleenex and laid the cricket on it. Then he took another and started to dust him off. Ever so softly he tapped the hard black shell, and the antennae, and legs, and wings. Gradually the dirt that had collected on the insect fell away. His true color was still black, but now it had a bright, glossy **sheen**.

sheen: shine

When Mario had cleaned off the cricket as much as he could, he hunted around the floor of the station for a matchbox. In a minute he'd found one and knocked out one end. Then he folded a sheet of Kleenex, tucked it in the box and put the cricket in. It made a perfect bed. The cricket seemed to like his new home. He moved around a few times and settled himself comfortably.

Mario sat for a time, just looking. He was so happy and excited that when anyone walked through the station, he forgot to shout "Newspapers!" and "Magazines!"

Then a thought occurred to him: perhaps the cricket was hungry. He **rummaged** through his jacket pocket and found a piece of a chocolate bar that had been left over from supper. Mario broke off one corner and held it out to the cricket on the end of his finger. Cautiously the insect lifted his head to the chocolate. He seemed to smell it a moment, then took a bit. A shiver of pleasure went over Mario as the cricket ate from his hand.

rummaged: searched

Mama and Papa Bellini came up the stairs from the lower level of the station. Mama was a short woman—a little stouter than she liked to admit—who wheezed and got a red face when she had to climb steps. Papa was tall and somewhat bent over, but he had a kindness that shone about him. There seemed always to be something smiling inside Papa. Mario was so busy feeding his cricket that he didn't see them when they came up to the newsstand.

"So?" said Mama, craning over the counter. "What now?"

"I found a cricket!" Mario exclaimed. He picked the insect up very gently between his thumb and forefinger and held him out for his parents to see.

Mama studied the little black creature carefully. "It's a bug," she pronounced finally. "Throw it away."

Mario's happiness fell in ruins. "No, Mama," he said anxiously. "It's a special kind of bug. Crickets are good luck."

"Good luck, ay?" Mama's voice had a way of sounding very dry when she didn't believe something. "**Cricketers** are good luck—so I suppose ants are better luck. And cockroaches are the best luck of all. Throw it away."

cricketers: crickets

"Please, Mama, I want to keep him for a pet."

"No bugs are coming to my house," said Mama. "We've got enough already with the screens full of holes. He'll whistle to his friends—they'll come from all over—we'll have a houseful of cricketers."

"No we won't," said Mario in a low voice. "I'll fix the screens." But he knew it was no use arguing with Mama. When she had made up her mind, you might as well try to reason with the Eighth Avenue subway.

"How was selling tonight?" asked Papa. He was a peaceful man and always tried to head off arguments. Changing the subject was something he did very well.

"Fifteen papers and four magazines," said Mario. "And Paul just bought a *Sunday Times*."

"No one took a *Musical America*, or anything else nice?" Papa was very proud that his newsstand carried all of what he called the "quality magazines."

"No," answered Mario.

"So you spend less time playing with cricketers, you'll sell more papers," said Mama.

"Oh now, now," Papa soothed her. "Mario couldn't help it if nobody buys."

"You can tell the temperature with crickets, too," said Mario. "You count the number of chirps in a minute, divide by four and add forty. They're very intelligent."

"Who needs a cricketer-thermometer?" said Mama. "It's coming on summer, it's New York—it's hot. And how do you know so much about cricketers? Are you one?"

"Jimmy Lebovski told me last summer," said Mario.

"Then give it to the expert Jimmy Lebovski," said Mama. "Bugs carry germs. He doesn't come in the house."

Mario looked down at his new friend in the palm of his hand. Just for once he had been really happy. The cricket seemed to know that something was wrong. He jumped onto the shelf and crept into the matchbox.

"He could keep it here in the newsstand," suggested Papa.

Mario jumped at that idea. "Yes, and then he wouldn't have to come home. I could feed him here, and leave him here, and you'd never have to see him," he said to Mama. "And when you took the stand, I'd bring him with me."

Mama paused. "Cricketer," she said **scornfully**. "What do we want with a cricketer?"

scornfully: with disgust

"What do we want with a newsstand?" said Papa. "We got it—let's keep it." There was something **resigned**, but nice, about Papa.

resigned: to have given up

"You said I could have a dog," said Mario, "but I never got him. And I never got a cat, or a bird, or anything. I wanted this cricket for my pet."

"He's yours then," said Papa. And when Papa spoke in a certain quiet tone—that was all there was to it. Even Mama didn't dare disagree.

She took a deep breath. "Oh well—" she sighed. And Mario knew it would be all right. Mama's saying "oh well" was her way of giving in. "But only on trial he stays. At the first sign of the cricketer friends, or if we come down with **peculiar** diseases— out he goes!"

peculiar: odd

"Yes, Mama, anything you say," said Mario.

"Come on, Mario," Papa said. "Help me close up."

Mario held the matchbox up to his eye. He was sure the cricket looked much happier, now that he could stay. "Goodnight," he said. "I'll be back in the morning."

"Talking to it yet!" said Mama. "I've got a cricketer for a son."

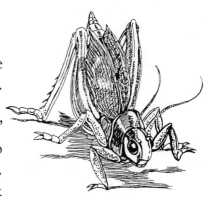

Papa took one side of the cover to the newsstand, Mario the other, and together they fitted it on. Papa locked it down. As they were going downstairs to the trains, Mario looked back over his shoulder. He could almost feel the cricket, snugged away in his matchbox bed, in the darkness.

Mario keeps the cricket in a cage in his parents' newsstand in Times Square. At night, when no people are around, the cricket becomes friends with a cat and a rat. The cricket later becomes famous as the "Singing Cricket of Times Square."

Source: George Selden, *The Cricket in Times Square*. New York: Farrar, Straus & Giroux, Inc. 1960.

City, City

by Marci Ridlon

If you have ever lived in a city, you know that there are both good sides and bad sides to living there. In the poem below, how does Marci Ridlon express both the good sides and bad sides of urban life?

I

City, city,

Wrong and bad,

Looms above me

When I'm sad,

Throws its shadow

On my care,

Sheds its poison

In my air,

Pounds me with its

Noisy fist,

Sprays me with its

Sooty mist.

Till, with sadness

On my face,

I long to live

Another place.

II

City, city,

Golden-clad,

Shines around me

When I'm glad,

Lifts me with its

Strength and height,

Fills me with its

Sound and sight,

Takes me to its

Crowded heart,

Holds me so I

Won't depart.

Till, with gladness

On my face,

I wouldn't live

Another place.

golden-clad: dressed in gold

looms: towers

sooty: covered with ashes

What do you like about the type of community you live in? What do you dislike? You might like to write a two-part poem about the good sides and bad sides of living in a rural or suburban neighborhood.

Source: Marci Ridlon, *That Was Summer.* New York: Follett Publishing Company, 1969.

52

UNIT 3

THE SOUTHEAST

*And He's allowed me to go up
to the mountain. And I've
looked over. And I've seen
the promised land.*

Dr. Martin Luther King, Jr.
civil rights leader

KNOXVILLE, TENNESSEE

by Nikki Giovanni

What do you think of when you think about summer? Perhaps you think of vacation, swimming, baseball, and enough sunshine to be able to play outdoors after dinner. Poet Nikki Giovanni remembers her summers in Knoxville, Tennessee. What are some of the reasons that summer is her favorite season?

I always like summer

best

you can eat fresh corn

from daddy's garden

and okra

and greens

and cabbage

and lots of barbecue

and buttermilk

and homemade ice cream

at the church picnic

and listen to

gospel music

outside

at the church

homecoming

and go to the mountains
  with

your grandmother

and go barefooted

and be warm

all the time

not only when you go
  to bed

and sleep

Which season do you like best? If you wrote a poem about that season, what things would you include?

Source: Nikki Giovanni, *Black Feeling Black Talk Black Judgement*. New York: William Morrow & Company, Inc., 1968.

When I Was Young in the Mountains

by Cynthia Rylant

Cynthia Rylant grew up in the Appalachian Mountains, in Cool Ridge, West Virginia. Her grandfather was a coal miner, and they lived in a small house with no running water. Times may have been tough, but her memories are of a simple, happy life. Rylant remembers little things with great joy, like swimming in a swimming hole and pumping water from a well. Her memories are from a different time, the 1950s. Many things have changed since the way of life that Rylant remembers. But life in the Appalachian Mountains is still different from life in a city. How do you think that living in the mountains affects a person's way of life?

*W*hen I was young in the mountains, Grandfather came home in the evening covered with the black dust of a coal mine. Only his lips were clean, and he used them to kiss the top of my head.

When I was young in the mountains, Grandmother spread the table with hot corn bread, pinto beans and fried okra. Later, in the middle of the night, she walked through the grass with me to the **johnny-house** and held my hand in the dark. I promised never to eat more than one serving of okra again.

When I was young in the mountains, we walked across the cow pasture and through the woods, carrying our towels. The swimming hole was dark and muddy, and we sometimes saw snakes, but we jumped in anyway. On our way home, we stopped at Mr. Crawford's for a mound of white butter. Mr. Crawford and Mrs. Crawford looked alike and always smelled of sweet milk.

When I was young in the mountains, we pumped pails of water from the well at the bottom of the hill, and heated the water to fill round tin tubs for our baths. Afterwards we stood in front of the old black stove, shivering and giggling, while Grandmother heated cocoa on top.

When I was young in the mountains, we went to church in the schoolhouse on Sundays, and sometimes walked with the **congregation** through the cow pasture to the dark swimming hole, for **baptism**. My cousin Peter was laid back into the water, and his white shirt stuck to him, and my Grandmother cried.

johnny-house: an outdoor bathroom

congregation: the people who belong to a church

baptism: a religious ceremony in which a person is sprinkled with water

When I was young in the mountains, we listened to frogs sing at dusk and awoke to cowbells outside our windows. Sometimes a black snake came in the yard, and my Grandmother would threaten it with a hoe. If it did not leave, she used the hoe to kill it. Four of us once **draped** a very long snake, dead of course, across our necks for a photograph.

draped: hung

When I was young in the mountains, we sat on the porch swing in the evenings, and Grandfather sharpened my pencils with his pocket knife. Grandmother sometimes shelled beans and sometimes braided my hair. The dogs lay around us, and the stars sparkled in the sky. A bob white whistled in the forest. Bob-bob-bob white!

When I was young in the mountains, I never wanted to go to the ocean, and I never wanted to go the desert. I never wanted to go anywhere else in the world, for I was in the mountains. And that was always enough.

Today you probably swim in a pool and get your water from a faucet. But you may also find pleasure from some simple things. What are some of the things you enjoy about your everyday life? How do you think you'll remember them when you grow up?

Source: Cynthia Rylant, *When I Was Young in the Mountains*. New York: E. P. Dutton, 1982.

John Henry

Traditional Ballad

In 1869 the eastern and western parts of the United States were finally connected by railroad. Thousands of miles of railroad tracks were laid down by strong men like the legendary John Henry, a steel driller on the C & O Railroad in the early 1870s. During this period, railroad companies began using machines to do some of the work performed by men. The story has it that John Henry died trying to beat a steam drill in a race to dig the Big Bend Tunnel in West Virginia. Songs and stories spread across the country, describing John Henry's strength and courage and his determination to beat that steam drill. Why do you think it was so important to John Henry to beat the machine?

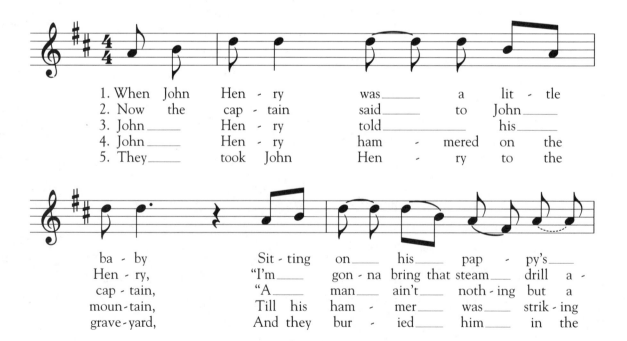

1. When John Hen - ry was a lit - tle ba - by
2. Now the cap - tain said to John Hen - ry,
3. John Hen - ry told his cap - tain,
4. John Hen - ry ham - mered on the moun-tain,
5. They took John Hen - ry to the grave-yard,

Sit - ting on his pap - py's
"I'm gon - na bring that steam drill a -
"A man ain't noth - ing but a
Till his ham - mer was strik - ing
And they bur - ied him in the

Source: Edith Fowke and Joe Glazer, *Songs of Work and Protest*. New York: Dover Publications, 1973.

Go Free or Die

by Jeri Ferris

Harriet Tubman was born into slavery on a plantation in Maryland in 1820. From the age of six, she chopped wood and hoed fields with the other enslaved people. Her owners frequently whipped her to make her work even harder. When Harriet was around 11 years old she began to hear other slaves whispering about an escape road to the North, to freedom. She vowed that one day she would "go free or die." Finally, when she was 28 years old, Tubman decided that the time had come. She set off early one morning on the "underground railroad." Like many other enslaved people, Tubman was helped by kind people along the way who gave her rides in wagons or on horses or hid her in their homes. In the following selection from her biography, Harriet Tubman is on the final stretch leading to freedom. It is also the most dangerous. How does Tubman feel as she gets closer to freedom?

Now she was alone again, with only the North Star to show her the way. It was a warm night. The gentle wind wrapped her in its soft breath. Harriet heard it whispering through the woods. She walked north all night, and when morning came, she found a hiding place in the hollow of a tree. Harriet rested there, hidden from the slave catchers, until the sun went down.

As darkness crept through the woods on the second night, Harriet watched for the stars to appear in the sky before she started north again. "I'm getting close to freedom, Lord, I know I am," she said as she pushed through the bushes and clumps of grass.

Hours later Harriet came to a graveyard at the edge of the woods. She saw a man walking among the tombstones, and her heart almost stopped. Was he a ghost? Was he a slave catcher? Hiding in the tall weeds, she silently moved closer. The man was talking to himself. "I have the ticket for the railroad," he said. "I have the ticket for the railroad." Harriet stood up and walked toward him.

"Harriet?" he asked in a friendly voice. "I've been waiting for you. Hurry now, before it gets too light." He handed her a shovel and a pile of workman's clothes: a hat, heavy shoes, and overalls to go over her long dress.

"I'm Mr. Trent, Harriet. You're going to walk into Wilmington as my workman. We'll pass guards watching the road for runaway slaves, but just follow me and don't say a word."

Soon Harriet was ready. Her bandanna and scarf were hidden under the workman's hat. She put the shovel over her shoulder and walked behind Mr. Trent toward the bridge that led to Wilmington. Harriet saw groups of men standing by the road looking closely at every black person who passed. At the entrance to the bridge, guards waited on horseback. Harriet's heart pounded so hard she thought the slave catchers would hear it, but after one look, they paid no attention to Mr. Trent and his helper.

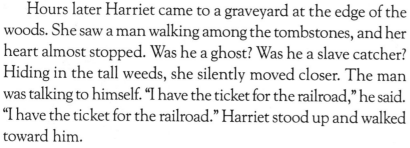

Harriet followed Mr. Trent into Wilmington. She had never seen such a busy, noisy town before. The roads were filled with horses and buggies and people hurrying here and there. Big square buildings seemed to push in at her from both sides of the long streets. They walked on through the town until Mr. Trent stopped in front of a small shop. The owner of the shop, Thomas Garrett, was expecting Harriet.

As Mr. Trent said good-bye, he warned Harriet to take great care. "It's very dangerous here, Harriet, because this is the last town before you reach the free state of Pennsylvania. Slave catchers are watching to be sure no runaway slaves cross the line into Pennsylvania. But with God's help, you will soon be free!"

Harriet rested for a day in Mr. Garrett's home. Then on Sunday, she dressed in new clothes. "Many people want to see the slaves go free, Harriet," Mr. Garrett told her. "These people provide clothes for runaway slaves to wear." Harriet put on a hat with a long veil that covered her face. Then Mr. Garrett helped her into his buggy. As their horse trotted through town, they looked as if they were just taking a Sunday drive. No one would know that the well-dressed lady in the buggy was really a runaway slave.

When they reached the wooded countryside north of Wilmington, Mr. Garrett stopped the horse. "I must turn back here, Harriet. No one is watching just now, but be very careful. sign at the crossroad. Look for this word." He gave her a paper with Pennsylvania printed on it. "That sign marks the line between the slave states of the South and the free states of the North. Then go straight down the road to Philadelphia, the

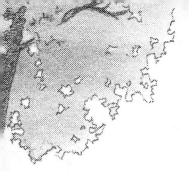

first big town in Pennsylvania." Mr. Garrett smiled at Harriet. "God surely has sent a special angel of mercy to keep thee safe all this way. Thou art almost free!"

Mr. Garrett's buggy turned back toward Wilmington. Harriet stood for a minute, looking at the empty road in front of her. Soon she would be free! As she headed North, her feet seemed as light as angel's wings. On she ran, looking for the wooden sign.

Suddenly she felt afraid. It was too dangerous to be out on the road. She turned and ran into the woods. Moments later two horsemen galloped past, shouting and laughing. Then the road was quiet again, but Harriet stayed in the shadowy woods.

Harriet ran until she saw a crossroad ahead. There was a small sign on a post by the side of the road. The letters on the sign were the same as the letters on the paper in her hand. Slowly she left the safety of the trees and walked until she could touch the warm wood of the little sign that marked her freedom. "Thank you, Lord," she whispered, kneeling on the ground. "You brought me safely here." Harriet wiped the tears from her face. She looked at her hands to see if she was still the same person, now that she was free.

At last Harriet got to her feet and stood in the middle of the road. "Oh, Lord, look! There's such a glory over everything. The sun looks like gold on the fields. I feel as if I'm in heaven!" Harriet sang and cried for joy as she walked down that free road toward Philadelphia.

"I'm free. I'm free at last!"

Harriet Tubman escaped to freedom in 1848. Her new friends in the North warned her that she must never return to the South, but Tubman would not settle for her own freedom. She wanted to help her family and other people escape from slavery as well. Over and over again, Tubman risked her life to help others go free. Between 1848 and 1861, she made 19 trips south. She helped more than 300 slaves escape to freedom—including her three brothers and her parents! Many people called her "Moses" because, like Moses in the Bible, Harriet Tubman led her people to freedom.

Source: Jeri Ferris, *Go Free or Die: A Story About Harriet Tubman*. Minneapolis: Carolrhoda Books, Inc., 1988.

The Riddle Tale of Freedom

by Virginia Hamilton

When enslaved African Americans were working in the fields together, they often told stories, riddles, and jokes to help pass the long, hard days. Some of their stories contained puzzles within them, and so they have become known as "riddle tales." Virginia Hamilton has studied African-American riddles and tales and collected them in a book called **The People Could Fly.** *She tried to write the stories using the same words that the people who first told them might have used. The story below is about a topic that comes up in many of the tales—freedom. In riddle tales, solving a riddle or asking a good riddle leads to freedom. Why do you think so many of the slave stories and riddles were about freedom?*

Now here it **tis.** Long time ago, there was a slave and a slaveowner. They got along. They liked to joke back and forth sometimes. Those two would exchange jokes and riddles. The slave man say, "**Mas**, you give me a riddle today and I figured it out. Now, tomorrow, I'll give you one."

tis: old-fashioned way to say "is"

Mas: Master

"All right," the slaveowner says, "you bring me one in the mornin'. "

"And if you can't figure it," said the slave, "you give me my freedom in the mornin', too."

So that was the deal. The mornin' come. The slave goes to the owner's place. Owner says, "Come on in. I heard you comin'. Come on in. You got that riddle with you you said you'd bring me?"

"Sure do," said the slave. His old dog had died the night before. The dog's name was Love. The slave took a piece of

Love's skin and wrapped it around his right hand. So the slave says, "I've got you a riddle right here."

"Well, go ahead," said the owner, "tell it to me."

"Well, then, here," said the slave. And he told the riddle like this:

> "Love I see; Love I stand.
> Love I holds in my right hand."

"Now what is the answer, Mas?" asked the slave.

The slaveowner thought a long time. He tried to guess the riddle, but he just couldn't figure it out.

"Well, I give up," the slaveowner said. "So I have to give you your freedom because I said I would if I couldn't guess. But first, tell me what the answer is."

"Well, here it tis," said the slave. "See, wrapped around my right hand? That's my dead dog's skin, and his name was Love. Well, I was standin' right here with it and I had it in my hand, just seein' it. So that's why I tell the riddle:

> "Love I see; Love I stand.
> Love I holds in my right hand."

That's how the riddle gave the slave his freedom.

Another slave riddle went like this: "Were twelve pears hanging high, and twelve pears hanging low. Twelve kings came riding by. Each took a pear, and how many were left hanging there?" The answer was 23. To begin with there were 24. One of the kings, whose name was Each, took one! What riddles do you and your friends like to tell?

Source: Virginia Hamilton, *The People Could Fly*. New York: Alfred Knopf, Inc., 1985.

Battle Cry of Freedom

Civil War Battle Song

Northern Version by George F. Root, 1861   **Southern Version by W. H. Barnes, 1861**

When the Civil War began in 1861, songwriters rushed to write songs for soldiers to sing. One of the most popular songs to sweep the North was George F. Root's "Battle Cry of Freedom." Union troops sang it in camp, in battle, and when marching. The tune was so catchy that Confederate troops also began singing it—but they, of course, wanted different words. So a Southerner named W. H. Barnes wrote a new version for the South. How do the two versions reveal two different perspectives?

Spirited

North: 1. Yes we'll ral - ly 'round the flag, boys, we'll
South: 1. Our _____ flag is proud - ly float-ing, On the

ral - ly once a - gain, Shout - ing the bat - tle cry of
land and on the main, Shout, shout the bat - tle cry of

Free - dom, We will ral - ly from the hill - side, we'll
Free - dom; Be - neath it oft we've con-quered, And will

gath - er from the plain, Shout - ing the bat - tle cry of Free - dom.
con - quer oft a - gain, Shout, shout the bat - tle cry of Free - dom.

Chorus

North: The Un - ion for - ev - er, Hur - rah, boys, Hur - rah!
South: Our Dix - ie for - ev - er, she's nev-er at a loss;

Down with the trai - tor, Up with the star; While we
Down with the ea - gle, Up with the cross. We'll____

ral - ly 'round the flag, boys, Ral - ly once a - gain.
ral - ly 'round the bon-ny flag, we'll ral - ly once a - gain.

Shout - ing the bat - tle cry of Free - dom. Free - dom.
Shout, shout the bat - tle cry of Free - dom. Free - dom.

North:

2. We are springing to the call
   Of our brothers gone before,
     Shouting the battle cry of Freedom,
   And we'll fill the vacant ranks
   With a million Free men more,
     Shouting the battle cry of Freedom.

   Chorus

3. We will welcome to our numbers
   The loyal, true and brave,
     Shouting the battle cry of Freedom,
   And although he may be poor
   He shall never be a slave,
     Shouting the battle cry of Freedom.

   Chorus

4. So we're springing to the call
   From the East and from the West,
     Shouting the battle cry of Freedom,
   And we'll hurl the rebel crew
   From the land we love the best,
     Shouting the battle cry of Freedom.

   Chorus

South:

2. Our gallant boys have marched
   To the rolling of the drums,
     Shout, shout the battle cry of Freedom;
   And the leaders in charge
   Cry, "Come boys, come!"
     Shout, shout the battle cry of Freedom.

   Chorus

3. They have laid down their lives
   On the bloody battle field,
     Shout, shout the battle cry of Freedom;
   Their motto is resistance—
   "To tyrants we'll not yield!"
     Shout, shout the battle cry of Freedom.

   Chorus

4. While our boys have responded
   And to the field have gone,
     Shout, shout the battle cry of Freedom;
   Our noble women also
   Have aided them at home.
     Shout, shout the battle cry of Freedom.

   Chorus

Source: Paul Glass and Louis Singer, *Singing Soldiers: A History of the Civil War in Song.*
New York: Da Capo Press, 1975.

Rosa Parks: My Story

by Rosa Parks

For many years African Americans in the south had been forced by law to sit in separate sections of trains and buses. Most blacks opposed these unfair laws, and on December 1, 1955, a woman in Montgomery, Alabama, decided to do something about them. What did Rosa Parks do? Parks tells you herself in the following selection from her autobiography. In what ways does she show courage?

When I got off from work that evening of December 1, I went to Court Square as usual to catch the Cleveland Avenue bus home. I didn't look to see who was driving when I got on, and by the time I recognized him, I had already paid my fare. It was the same driver who had put me off the bus back in 1943, twelve years earlier. He was still tall and heavy, with red, rough-looking skin. And he was still mean-looking. I didn't know if he had been on that route before—they switched the drivers around sometimes. I do know that most of the time if I saw him on a bus, I wouldn't get on it.

I saw a **vacant** seat in the middle section of the bus and took it. I didn't even question why there was a vacant seat even though there were quite a few people standing in the back. If I had thought about it at all, I would probably have figured maybe someone saw me get on and did not take the seat but left it vacant for me. There was a man sitting next to the window and two women across the aisle.

vacant: empty

The next stop was the Empire Theater, and some whites got on. They filled up the white seats, and one man was left standing. The driver looked back at us. He said, "Let me have

68

those front seats," because they were the front seats of the black section. Didn't anybody move. We just sat where we were, the four of us. Then he spoke a second time: "Y'all better **make it light** on yourselves and let me have those seats."

make it light: make it easier

The man in the window seat next to me stood up, and I moved to let him pass by me, and then I looked across the aisle and saw that the two women were also standing. I moved over to the window seat. I could not see how standing up was going to "make it light" for me. The more we gave in and complied, the worse they treated us. . . .

People always say that I didn't give up my seat because I was tired, but that isn't true. I was not tired physically, or no more tired than I usually was at the end of a working day. I was not old, although some people have an image of me as being old then. I was forty-two. No, the only tired I was, was tired of giving in.

The driver of the bus saw me still sitting there, and he asked was I going to stand up. I said, "No." He said, "Well, I'm going to have you arrested." Then I said, "You may do that." These were the only words we said to each other. I didn't even know his name, which was James Blake, until we were in court together. He got out of the bus and stayed outside for a few minutes, waiting for the police.

In the 1950s African Americans were forced by law to sit separately, in the back of the bus.

Rosa Parks takes a seat where she chooses, one year after her historic protest which led to the end of segregation on public transportation.

As I sat there, I tried not to think about what might happen. I knew that anything was possible. I could be **manhandled** or beaten. I could be arrested. People have asked me if it occurred to me then that I could be the test case the **NAACP** had been looking for. I did not think about that at all. In fact if I had let myself think too deeply about what might happen to me, I might have gotten off the bus. But I chose to remain.

manhandled: treated roughly

NAACP: National Association for the Advancement of Colored People, an organization that works for civil rights

Rosa Parks was arrested and put into jail. Word spread quickly throughout the African-American community and people were very angry. They, too, were tired of giving in. Led by Dr. Martin Luther King, Jr., African Americans joined together and refused to ride the city buses at all. Finally, a year later, the segregation laws were changed. Rosa Parks has spent the rest of her life working for civil rights for all people. "Everyone living together in peace and harmony and love," she writes, ". . . that's the goal that we seek."

Source: Rosa Parks, *Rosa Parks: My Story.* New York: Dial Books, 1992.

I See the Promised Land

by Dr. Martin Luther King, Jr., 1968

Rosa Parks's decision not to give up her bus seat helped give other people the courage to fight for civil rights. One of the greatest leaders of this movement was a young minister named Dr. Martin Luther King, Jr. During the 1950s and 1960s, Dr. King led many marches and demonstrations for civil rights. Like many great leaders, King faced danger from people who weren't ready for change. In 1968, King spoke about the struggles and successes he had seen. In the final part of the speech, printed below, King explains why he is no longer afraid of being killed. What do you think he means by "the promised land"?

Well, I don't know what will happen now. We've got some difficult days ahead. But it doesn't matter with me now. Because I've been to the mountaintop. And I don't mind. Like anybody, I would like to live a long life. **Longevity** has its place. But I'm not concerned about that now. I just want to do God's will. And He's allowed me to go up to the mountain. And I've looked over. And I've seen the promised land. I may not get there with you. But I want you to know tonight, that we, as a people, will get to the promised land. And I'm happy, tonight. I'm not worried about anything. I'm not fearing any man. Mine eyes have seen the glory of the coming of the Lord.

longevity: living long

While King predicted that he might be killed before his goals were reached, he could not have known the end would come so soon. The day after this speech, April 4, 1968, King was murdered, and the civil rights movement lost its greatest leader. His words, however, have helped to keep the movement alive. Do you think that we have reached King's "promised land" yet?

Source: James Melvin Washington, *A Testament of Hope: The Essential Writings of Martin Luther King, Jr.* San Francisco: Harper & Row, Publishers, 1986.

I Hear America Singing

by Walt Whitman, 1856

Walt Whitman was a schoolteacher, a nurse in the Civil War, a newspaper reporter, a clerk for the United States government, and also a famous American poet! Whitman's poems celebrated the common man in America—regular people like workers and parents and immigrants. Who are the Americans that he hears singing in "I Hear America Singing"?

I hear America singing, the varied carols I hear,
Those of mechanics, each one singing his as it should be
    blithe and strong,
The carpenter singing his as he measures his plank or
    beam,
The **mason** singing his as he makes ready for work, or
    leaves off work,
The boatman singing what belongs to him in his boat, the
    deck-hand singing on the steamboat deck.
The shoemaker singing as he sits on his bench, the hatter
    singing as he stands,
The wood-cutter's song, the **ploughboy**'s on his way in the
    morning or at noon intermission or at sundown,
The delicious singing of the mother, or of the young wife
    at work, or of the girl sewing or washing,
Each singing what belongs to him or her and to none else,
The day what belongs to the day—at night the party of
    young fellows, **robust**, friendly,
Singing with open mouths their strong **melodious** songs.

blithe: happy

mason: someone who builds with stone

ploughboy: boy who plows fields on a farm

robust: strong, healthy
melodious: tuneful

Walt Whitman heard many of the different voices that make America sing. On the next page you will read about one person who felt his voice had not been heard.

Source: Walt Whitman, *Leaves of Grass*. Brooklyn, NY: Fowler and Wells, 1856.

I, Too

by Langston Hughes, 1925

Langston Hughes was born in Joplin, Missouri, in 1902, ten years after poet Walt Whitman's death. Hughes grew up admiring Whitman's poetry about ordinary people. However, Hughes felt that one group's "songs" were not being heard: African Americans. So in 1925 Hughes sat down and wrote his own poem, "I, Too." How would you compare Walt Whitman's and Langston Hughes's views of America?

I, too, sing America.
I am the darker brother.
They send me to eat in the kitchen
When company comes,
But I laugh,
And eat well,
And grow strong.
Tomorrow,
I'll be at the table
When company comes.
Nobody'll dare
Say to me,
"Eat in the kitchen,"
Then.
Besides,
They'll see how beautiful I am
And be ashamed—
I, too, am America.

Langston Hughes's poem became as famous as Walt Whitman's. But many people had to work for civil rights to make Hughes's hope for "tomorrow" come true.

Source: Langston Hughes, *The Selected Poems of Langston Hughes*. New York: Alfred A. Knopf, 1925.

Puerto Rico

by Eileen Figueroa

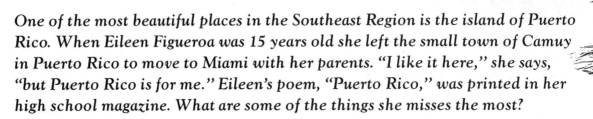

One of the most beautiful places in the Southeast Region is the island of Puerto Rico. When Eileen Figueroa was 15 years old she left the small town of Camuy in Puerto Rico to move to Miami with her parents. "I like it here," she says, "but Puerto Rico is for me." Eileen's poem, "Puerto Rico," was printed in her high school magazine. What are some of the things she misses the most?

Puerto Rico, isla del Caribe
La más bella es por cierto
Con sus palmares y sus vientos,
Acaricia a todo aquel
que en esta isla se encuentra.

Los atardeceres en mi Borinquen
son muy tranquilos y serenos
puedes oír los coqúies
cómo cantan a lo lejos.

Querido Puerto Rico
no sabes lo mucho que lo siento
El haber tenido que dejarte
para mí es un dolor immenso.

Pero sé que algún día he de volver
a esta tierra tan querida
que llenó mis días de alegrías
y que mi corazón aún no olvida.

Puerto Rico, certainly the most beautiful
Caribbean island
With palm trees and breezes,
it caresses everyone
found on the island.

Dusk on my island
is so very tranquil and serene
you can hear the coquís
singing in the distance.

Beloved Puerto Rico
you don't know how sorry I am
Having to leave you
is still a source of great pain.

But I know that some day
I'll return
to this cherished land
that filled my days with joy
and that my heart cannot forget.

After she finishes high school, Eileen plans to go to college in Puerto Rico. What things would you miss if you moved to another place?

Source: Eileen Figueroa, "Puerto Rico." Miami, FL: *Search II Magazine*, 1991.

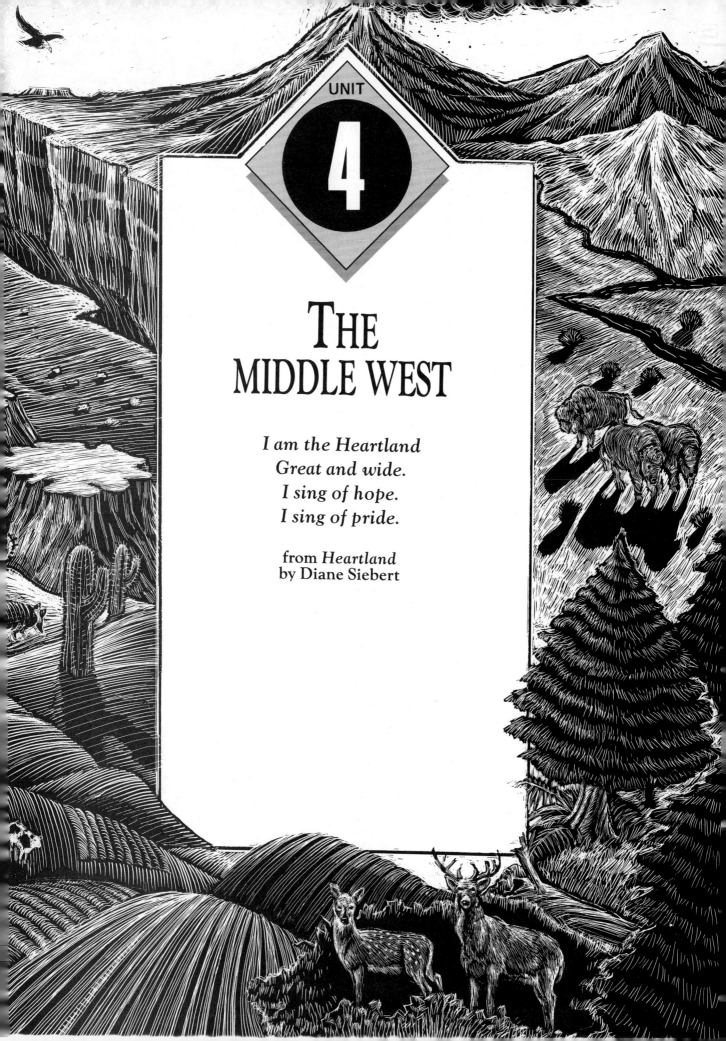

UNIT

4

THE
MIDDLE WEST

*I am the Heartland
Great and wide.
I sing of hope.
I sing of pride.*

from *Heartland*
by Diane Siebert

Heartland

by Diane Siebert

The food grown by American farmers feeds the people of the United States and many people around the world. In her poem "Heartland," Diane Siebert celebrates the farmers of the Middle West, their fields of corn and wheat, and their herds of cattle and sheep and pigs. Everyone in the United States benefits from the hard work of farmers. What have you eaten today that started out on a farm?

I am the Heartland.

Hear me speak

In voices raised by those who seek

To live their lives upon the land,

To know and love and understand

The secrets of a living earth—

Its strengths, its weaknesses, its worth;

Who, Heartland born and Heartland **bred,**   **bred:** raised

Possess the will to move ahead.

I am the Heartland.

I survive

To keep America, my home, alive.

I am the Heartland.

Smell the fields,

The rich, dark earth, and all it yields;

The air before a coming storm,

76

A newborn calf, so damp and warm;
The dusty grain in barns that hold
The bales of hay, all green and gold.
For I have learned of drought and hail,
Of floods and frosts and crops that fail,
And of tornadoes as they move . . .
In frightening paths, again to prove
That in the Heartland, on these plains,
Despite Man's power, Nature **reigns**.

reigns: rules

Before me, summer stretches out
With pastures **draped** in **lush**, green grass,
And as the days of growing pass,
I feel the joy when fields of grain
Are blessed by sunlight, warmth, and rain;
And winter, white and cold, **descends**
With blizzards howling as they sweep
Across me, piling snowdrifts deep.
Then days grow longer, skies turn clear,
And all the gifts of spring appear—
The young are born, the **seedlings** sprout;
      I am the Heartland:
        Earth and sky
And changing seasons passing by.
I feel the touch of autumn's chill,
And as its colors brightly spill
Across the land, the growing ends,
      I am the Heartland.
       In my song
Are cities beating, steady, strong,
With footsteps from a million feet
And sounds of traffic in the street;
Where giant mills and stockyards **sprawl**,
And neon-lighted shadows fall
From windowed walls of brick that rise

draped: covered
lush: thick

descends: falls

seedlings: young
   green plants

sprawl: stretch out

Toward the clouds, to scrape the skies;

Where highways meet and rails **converge**;

Where farm and city rhythms **merge**

To form a **vital** bond between

The concrete and the fields of green.

      I am the Heartland.

        On these plains

Rise elevators filled with grains.

They mark the towns where people walk

To see their neighbors, just to talk;

Where farmers go to get supplies

And sit a spell to **analyze**

The going price of corn and beans,

The rising cost of new machines;

Where steps are meant for shelling peas,

And kids build houses in the trees.

      I am the Heartland.

        On this soil

Live those who through the seasons **toil**:

The farmer, with his spirit strong;

The farmer, working hard and long,

A feed-and-seed-store cap in place,

Pulled down to shield a weathered face—

A face whose every crease and line

Can tell a tale, and help define

A lifetime spent beneath the sun,

A life of work that's never done.

By miles of wood and wire stretched

Around the barns and pastures where

The smell of **livestock** fills the air.

These are the farms where hogs are bred,

The farms where chicks are hatched and fed;

The farms where dairy cows are raised,

The farms where cattle herds are grazed;

converge: come together

merge: come together

vital: very important

analyze: think about

toil: work

livestock: farm animals

The farms with horses, farms with sheep—
Upon myself, all these I keep.
A patchwork quilt laid gently down
In hues of yellow, green, and brown
As tractors, plows, and planters go
Across my fields and, row by row,
Prepare the earth and plant the seeds
That grow to meet a nation's needs.
       I am the Heartland.
         I can feel

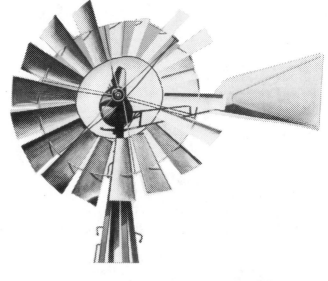

Machines of iron, tools of steel,
Creating farmlands, square by square—
A quilt of life I proudly wear:
       I am the Heartland.
        Shaped and lined
By rivers, great and small, that wind
Past farms, whose barns and silos stand
Like treasures in my fertile hand.
       I am the Heartland.
        Great and wide.
       I sing of hope.
       I sing of pride.
I am the land where wheat fields grow
In golden waves that **ebb and flow**;
Where cornfields stretched across the plains
Lie green between the country lanes.

ebb and flow: come in and out with the tides

The Middle West has some of the darkest, richest soil in the world. The region has sometimes been called the Corn Belt and sometimes the Breadbasket. Why do you think Diane Siebert calls it the Heartland?

Source: Diane Siebert, *Heartland*. New York: Thomas Y. Crowell, 1989.

SARAH PLAIN AND TALL

by Patricia MacLachlan

In the 1800s many people left the eastern coast of the United States to settle in regions to the west. In Patricia MacLachlan's historical novel, Sarah, Plain and Tall, a farmer named Jacob Witting is trying to make a home for his children in the Middle West region after the death of his wife. At that time there were very few women in the region so Jacob decides to find a wife in a surprising way. He advertises for one in the newspaper! A young woman named Sarah Wheaton from the coast of Maine answers his ad. In the following selection, Sarah has just arrived. She and the Wittings are getting to know each other to see if, indeed, she will become part of the family. The story is told from the point of view of Anna, the oldest daughter. What do the characters learn about each other and each other's region in the following selection?

The dogs loved Sarah first. Lottie slept beside her bed, curled in a soft circle, and Nick leaned his face on the covers in the morning, watching for the first sign that Sarah was awake. No one knew where Seal slept. Seal was a **roamer.**

Sarah's collection of shells sat on the windowsill.

"A scallop," she told us, picking up the shells one by one,

roamer: someone who wanders

"a sea clam, an oyster, a razor clam. And a conch shell. If you put it to your ear you can hear the sea." She put it to **Caleb**'s ear, then mine. Papa listened, too. Then Sarah listened once more, with a look so sad and far away that Caleb leaned against me.

Caleb: Anna's younger brother

"At least Sarah can hear the sea," he whispered.

Papa was quiet and shy with Sarah, and so was I. But Caleb talked to Sarah from morning until the light left the sky.

"Where are you going?" he asked. "To do what?"

"To pick flowers," said Sarah. "I'll hang some of them upside down and dry them so they'll keep some color. And we can have flowers all winter long."

"I'll come, too!" cried Caleb. "Sarah said winter," he said to me. "That means Sarah will stay."

Together we picked flowers, **paintbrush** and clover and prairie violets. There were buds on the wild roses that climbed up the **paddock** fence.

paintbrush: a red and orange wildflower

paddock: a small field where horses are kept

"The roses will bloom in early summer," I told Sarah. I looked to see if she knew what I was thinking. Summer was when the wedding would be. Might be. Sarah and Papa's wedding.

We hung the flowers from the ceiling in little bunches. "I've never seen this before," said Sarah. "What is it called?"

"Bride's bonnet," I told her.

Caleb smiled at the name.

"We don't have this by the sea," she said. "We have seaside goldenrod and wild asters and woolly ragwort."

"Woolly ragwort!" Caleb whooped. He made up a song.

"Woolly ragwort all around,

Woolly ragwort on the ground.

Woolly ragwort grows and grows,

Woolly ragwort in your nose."

Sarah and Papa laughed, and the dogs lifted their heads and thumped their tails against the wood floor. Seal sat on a kitchen chair and watched us with yellow eyes.

We ate Sarah's stew, the late light coming through the windows. Papa had baked bread that was still warm from the fire.

"The stew is fine," said Papa.

"Ayuh." Sarah nodded. "The bread, too."

"What does 'ayuh' mean?" asked Caleb.

"In Maine it means yes," said Sarah. "Do you want more stew?"

"Ayuh," said Caleb.

"Ayuh," echoed my father.

After dinner Sarah told us about **William**. "He has a gray-and-white boat named Kittiwake." She looked out the window. "That is a small gull found way off the shore where William fishes. There are three aunts who live near us. They wear silk dresses and no shoes. You would love them."

"Ayuh," said Caleb.

"Does your brother look like you?" I asked.

"Yes," said Sarah. "He is plain and tall."

At dusk Sarah cut Caleb's hair on the front steps, gathering his curls and scattering them on the fence and ground. Seal batted some hair around the porch as the dogs watched.

"Why?" asked Caleb.

"For the birds," said Sarah. "They will use it for their nests. Later we can look for nests of curls."

"Sarah said 'later,'" Caleb whispered to me as we spread his hair about. "Sarah will stay."

Sarah cut Papa's hair, too. No one else saw, but I found him behind the barn, tossing the pieces of hair into the wind for the birds.

Sarah brushed my hair and tied it up in back with a rose velvet ribbon she had brought from Maine. She brushed hers long and free and tied it back, too, and we stood side by side looking into the mirror. I looked taller, like Sarah, and fair and thin. And with my hair pulled back I looked a little like her daughter. Sarah's daughter.

And then it was time for singing.

Sarah sang us a song we had never heard before as we sat on the porch, insects buzzing in the dark, the rustle of cows in the grasses. It was called "Sumer is Icumen in," and she taught it to us all, even Papa, who sang as if he had never stopped singing.

"Sumer is icumen in,

Lhude sing **cuccu!**"

"What is sumer?" asked Caleb. He said it "soomer," the way Sarah had said it.

Lhude: loud
cuccu: cuckoo bird

"Summer," said Papa and Sarah at the same time. Caleb and I looked at each other. Summer was coming.

"Tomorrow," said Sarah, "I want to see the sheep. You know, I've never touched one."

"Never?" Caleb sat up.

"Never," said Sarah. She smiled and leaned back in her chair. "But I've touched seals. Real seals. They are cool and slippery and they slide through the water like fish. They can cry and sing. And sometimes they bark, a little like dogs."

Sarah barked like a seal. And Lottie and Nick came running from the barn to jump up on Sarah and lick her face and make her laugh. Sarah stroked them and scratched their ears and it was quiet again.

"I wish I could touch a seal right now," said Caleb, his voice soft in the night.

"So do I," said Sarah. She sighed, then she began to sing the summer song again. Far off in a field, a **meadowlark** sang, too.

meadowlark: a song bird

Sarah and the Whitting family share many adventures during the winter and following summer. During this time, Sarah grows to love the children and Jacob. She agrees to marry him and make the Middle West her home. There were many "mail order brides" in the 1800s who went west to marry men whom they had never met. Although this may sound strange to us today, it was one of the many ways that people from one region came to live in another.

Source: Patricia MacLachlan, *Sarah, Plain and Tall*. New York: Harper & Row, 1985.

True Stories About Abraham Lincoln

by Ruth Belov Gross

There are so many stories about Abraham Lincoln that it is hard to choose just a few to describe the kind of boy that Lincoln was and the kind of man that he became. In her book True Stories About Abraham Lincoln, Ruth Belov Gross chose two dozen of her favorites and put them into her own words. They might or might not be completely "true stories," but they are certainly interesting! Included below are three of these stories. What do the stories tell about Lincoln's personality?

A Borrowed Book

Abe liked to read in bed at night. Every night he took a book up to bed with him and read by the light of a candle.

One night Abe was reading a book he had borrowed from a farmer. The book was a biography of George Washington. Abe read until his candle went out. Then he put the book away. He put it in a crack in the wall, between two logs.

That night it rained. The rain came right through the cracks in the wall. And by morning the farmer's book was soaking wet.

Abe didn't have any money to pay for the book. So he went to the farmer and said, "I'm a good worker. Let me work on your farm until I have paid you for the book."

Abe worked hard in the farmer's cornfield. He worked for three days. "You've done a good job," the farmer said, and he let Abe keep the book.

Abe went home with the book that night. He was happy to have another book of his own—especially a book about Washington. George Washington was one of his heroes.

Earning a Living

Abe was on his own now.

At first he earned his living by doing the things he knew how to do best—chopping wood and splitting rails.

After a while, Abe got a job on a boat. He went to New Orleans with a boat full of pork and corn and live hogs. When he came back to Illinois, he got a job in a store in the town of New Salem. He sold tea and eggs and shoes and tools and hats.

The store didn't have many customers. So Abe spent a lot of time sitting under a tree near the store, reading.

One day when Abe was working in the store, a lady paid him six cents too much. That night, after the store was closed, Abe walked three miles to the lady's house. He gave her the six cents. Then he walked home again.

Soon people began to call Abe Lincoln "Honest Abe."

Move Over!

Lawyers in Lincoln's day traveled from one law court to another. Usually they traveled by horse and buggy.

Abe Lincoln was driving his buggy down a narrow road one day when he met another buggy. The road was too narrow for two buggies. One of the two would have to move over.

Lincoln didn't want to move over. If he did, he would get stuck in the mud.

The other driver didn't want to get stuck in the mud, either. "Move over!" he called to Lincoln.

"Move over yourself," Lincoln said.

"I won't," said the other driver.

Very slowly, Lincoln got up in his seat. He looked very tall against the sky. He got taller and taller.

"If you don't move over," he said in a loud voice, "I'll tell you what I'll do."

"Please—please don't go any higher," the other driver said. "I'll move over." And he moved over—into the mud. "What would you have done if I hadn't moved over?" he asked.

"I would have moved over myself," Lincoln said, and he drove on.

Abraham Lincoln became one of our country's greatest Presidents. Do the stories you have just read help you understand the qualities that made Lincoln such a strong leader?

Source: Ruth Belov Gross, *True Stories About Abraham Lincoln*. New York: Scholastic, Inc., 1973.

The Buffalo Go

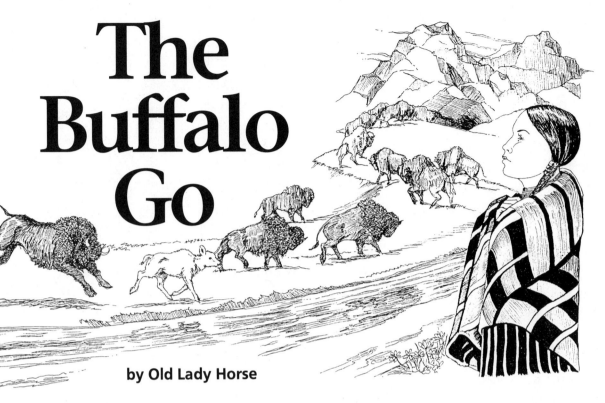

by Old Lady Horse

For hundreds of years giant herds of buffalo roamed the Great Plains of the Middle West. Many Indian groups, such as the Kiowa, depended on the buffalo for food, clothing, and shelter. In the late 1800s white hunters began killing all of the buffalo. In the legend below, a Kiowa woman named Old Lady Horse describes what happened to the buffalo and her people.

Everything the Kiowas had came from the buffalo. Their tepees were made of buffalo hides, so were their clothes and moccasins. They ate buffalo meat. Their containers were made of hide, or of bladders or stomachs. The buffalo were the life of the Kiowas.

Most of all, the buffalo was part of the Kiowa religion. A white buffalo calf must be sacrificed in the Sun Dance. The priests used part of the buffalo to make their prayers when they healed people or when they sang to the powers above.

So, when the white men wanted to build railroads, or when they wanted to farm or raise cattle, the buffalo still protected the Kiowas. They tore up the railroad tracks and the gardens. They chased the cattle off the ranges. The buffalo loved their people as much as the Kiowas loved them.

There was war between the buffalo and the white men. The white men built forts in the Kiowa country, and the . . . buffalo soldiers shot the buffalo as fast as they could, but the buffalo kept coming on, coming on, even into the post cemetery at Fort Sill. Soldiers were not enough to hold them back.

Then the white men hired hunters to do nothing but kill the buffalo. Up and down the plains those men ranged, shooting sometimes as many as a hundred buffalo a day. Behind them came the skinners with their wagons. They piled the hides and bones into the wagons until they were full, and then took their loads to the new railroad stations that were being built, to be shipped east to the market. Sometimes there would be a pile of bones as high as a man, stretching a mile along the railroad track.

The buffalo saw that their day was over. They could protect their people no longer. Sadly, the last **remnant** of the great herd gathered in council, and decided what they would do.

remnant: remaining part

The Kiowas were camped on the north side of Mount Scott, those of them who were still free to camp. One young woman got up very early in the morning. The dawn mist was still rising from Medicine Creek, and as she looked across the water, peering through the haze, she saw the last buffalo herd appear like a spirit dream.

Straight to Mount Scott the leader of the herd walked. Behind him came the cows and their calves, and the few young males who have survived. As the woman watched, the face of the mountain opened.

Inside Mount Scott the world was green and fresh, as it had been when she was a small girl. The rivers ran clear, not red. The wild plums were in blossom, chasing the red buds up the inside slopes. Into this world of beauty the buffalo walked, never to be seen again.

The next selection is a poem about the loss of the buffalo. As you read it, think about what these two pieces have in common.

Source: Alice Marriot and Carol K. Rachlin, *American Indian Mythology*. New York: Thomas Y. Crowell Company, 1968.

Buffalo Dusk

by Carl Sandburg

In 1878, when Carl Sandburg was born in Galesburg, Illinois, there were still buffalo roaming the prairies of North America. As Sandburg grew up, the Middle West changed. The Plain Indians, who had depended on the buffalo for survival, were forced onto reservations. The prairies were turned into farms. The towns grew into cities. By 1920, when Sandburg's poem "Buffalo Dusk" was published, almost all of the buffalo were gone. Dusk is the time of day just after sunset, when all of the sunlight disappears into darkness. Why do you think Carl Sandburg called this poem "Buffalo Dusk"?

The buffaloes are gone.

And those who saw the buffaloes are gone.

Those who saw the buffaloes by thousands and how they

    pawed the prairie **sod** into dust with their hoofs, their   **sod:** ground

    great heads down pawing on in a great **pageant** of dusk,   **pageant:** parade

Those who saw the buffaloes are gone.

And the buffaloes are gone.

Both Carl Sandburg and Old Lady Horse realized that the end of the buffalo had changed life in the Middle West forever. Today only a small number of buffalo still exists.

Source: Carl Sandburg, *Smoke and Steel*. New York: Harcourt Brace Jovanovich, 1920.

My Prairie Year

by Brett Harvey

In 1889, nine-year-old Elenore Plaisted and her family moved from Maine to the Dakotas as pioneers. When Elenore grew up, she wrote a memoir, recalling what life was like as a little girl on the prairie. Then 80 years later, Brett Harvey wrote a story based on her grandmother's memoir. As you will see, everyone in the pioneer home was expected to work hard, even the children. What different jobs did the family members have? What jobs do you have around your home?

Our house on the prairie was like a little white ship at sea. Not a tree, not a bush to be seen—just endless tall grass that **billowed** in the wind like the waves of an ocean. Our house was set on a small hill and around it was a pond made by rainwater, with a wooden bridge across it. The house was anchored to the ground with a high bank of earth that came up to the windowsills and was covered with grass. "To keep the house from blowing away in a tornado," Daddy said.

billowed: filled with air

Our family had come to the Dakotas from Maine to be what Daddy called "**homesteaders.**" Daddy came out first by himself to find our land and build our house. Then he sent for Mother and me and my little sister, Marjorie, and my baby brother, Billy. We traveled on a big, black train that **belched** smoke and steam. After what seemed like weeks, the train finally stopped one rainy night in a place called Andover. As we climbed down to the platform, there was Daddy, a black rubber figure stamping toward us, streaming with water and shouting happily, "Hallo! Em! Hallo, you children!"

homesteaders: people who built homes and farms on the prairies in the late 1800s

belched: let out suddenly and noisily

We felt very strange that first night in our new home. You could see right through the walls of our room, for they were made of pine boards which hadn't been plastered yet. Daddy nailed horse blankets over the bare boards, and Mother put

us to sleep on canvas cots. I fell asleep wondering what life would be like in this new place.

I learned that life on the prairie was different from life back home in Maine in every way.

Monday was washday. Mother learned to make a fire in the big kitchen range with soft, queer-smelling coal. My job was to trudge back and forth over the little wooden bridge, bringing back pail after pail of rainwater from our "**moat.**" Then Daddy would empty the buckets into the huge tin **washboiler** and hoist it up on the range to heat. After the clothes were washed, we emptied the washboiler and filled it up in the same way for rinsing.

moat: ditch filled with water

washboiler: old-fashioned washing machine

Later, Mother would carry the baskets, heavy with wet clothes, out to the clothesline. Marjorie and I would hand her things and she would hang them up. Then Marjorie and I would chase each other through the sweet-smelling sheets and clothes flapping in the sun, the damp ends brushing against our faces.

Tuesday was ironing and mending day. I stood on the soapbox by the ironing board, with my own little iron. It was heavy, but I was strong for my nine years. I ironed the handkerchiefs and towels, which I had sprinkled with water and rolled tight to keep damp.

In the afternoon, I sewed with Mother. Clothes seemed to wear out fast on the prairie and we were always darning stockings and mending underclothes. Mother showed me how to use a darning egg, but I didn't like staying indoors and envied Marjorie and Billy, who were still too young to sew.

On Wednesday we gardened in the morning before it got too hot. Mother had brought packets of seeds from New England, and we planted rows of peas, beets, tomatoes, beans, corn and melons. Watermelons were especially important in the heat of the summer. The water in our well was **tepid** and we ate watermelon to quench our thirst. No matter how hot it was, the melon always tasted cool and refreshing. We planted the corn in shallow **trenches** called drills. Things grew so fast on the prairie that in no time the corn shot up over my head. Then we children would play in the shady alleys between the stalks, decorating each other with soft, shining corn silk.

In the afternoons, Marjorie and I sat on boxes in the shade and did the lessons Mother had given us. Mother had to teach us herself because there was no school close enough for us to go to.

On Thursdays, Daddy and I would ride to Britton to get supplies. We had a funny, horse-drawn wagon with a round canvas top on hooks. Britton was two miles away on a straight road, black as ink. In town, the main street was either very muddy or deep with thick dust. You walked across it on a wobbly **boardwalk** of **planks**. The town was no more than a few shacks and a three-story wooden hotel, with six windows in rows of two up the face of it. The hotel **proprietor** had a daughter, Jennie, who was just my age, and we would sit on the back steps of the hotel and make doll clothes together.

Friday was cleaning day. Father had tried to get a woman from Britton to come and help Mother with the housework, but no one could be found. Women were scarce and needed

tepid: warm

trenches: long, narrow ditches

boardwalk: sidewalk
planks: wooden boards
proprietor: owner

in their own homes. So we all swept and scrubbed every corner of the house. Even Marjorie and baby Billy had jobs to do.

Saturday was cooking and baking day. All the bread that had been set to rise Friday night was **kneaded** into enough loaves for the week, and baked. Stacks and stacks of golden brown loaves were put out to cool on a table by the window. Then we wrapped them and packed them in the big wooden bread bin. We baked pans of ginger cookies and pies from dried apples and peaches because there was no fresh fruit on the prairie. In the summer we "**put up**" the vegetables from the garden. It was hot work, boiling the jars and the vegetables to keep everything clean. But after we were finished, our cellar cupboard was filled with brilliant jars of deep red beets, bright green and yellow beans, golden corn, and delicious, rosy watermelon pickles.

kneaded: mixed and pounded

put up: bottled

Sundays in the Dakotas were glorious. Sundays meant no work and no lesson except our Sunday School lesson. When that was over, we were free to run wild on the prairie. . . .

The Plaisteds and other pioneers had routines, with different tasks for each day of the week. Sometimes, however, things happened that kept them from their routines. You can read My Prairie Year *to find out what happened to Elenore and her family when a fire swept through the prairie. You can also read about how their homestead finally became their home.*

Source: Brett Harvey, *My Prairie Year.* New York: Holiday House, 1986.

LIFE ON THE PRAIRIE

with Laura Ingalls Wilder

Just like Elenore Plaisted, whom you read about on pages 90-93, Laura Ingalls Wilder grew up on the prairie in the late 1800. She later wrote eight books about her childhood adventures. Millions of people have grown up reading and loving the stories about the "little house on the prairie." Through her books, readers feel they have gotten to know the Ingalls family. Below are some pictures from Laura Ingalls Wilder's life. What do they show you about life on the prairie in the late 1800s?

In the first winter that the Ingalls family spent in De Smet, Minnesota, they were hit by a major blizzard. Sixty years later, Laura wrote a novel about that winter. She wrote in pencil on school paper. The first page of The Hard Winter *is shown at left.*

Even famous writers have to work hard on every word they write. Laura's novel was later published, but the title was changed to The Long Winter. *What similarities and differences can you see between the handwritten page and the words in the printed book?*

1. MAKE HAY WHILE THE SUN SHINES

THE MOWING machine's whirring sounded cheerfully from the old buffalo wallow south of the claim shanty, where bluestem grass stood thick and tall and Pa was cutting it for hay.

The sky was high and quivering with heat over the shimmering prairie. Half-way down to sunset, the sun blazed as hotly as at noon. The wind was scorching hot. But Pa had hours of mowing yet to do before he could stop for the night.

Laura drew up a pailful of water from the well at the edge of the Big Slough. She rinsed the brown jug till it was cool to her hand. Then she filled it with the fresh, cool water, corked it tightly, and started with it to the hayfield.

Swarms of little white butterflies hovered over the path. A dragon-fly with gauzy wings swiftly chased a

During "the long winter," Laura (right) and her sisters and her parents huddled around the stove in their little house, trying to keep warm. The photograph at right shows Laura and her sisters the year of that "hard winter."

The Youth's Companion was a much-loved children's magazine of short stories. Delivery of the magazine was stopped during bad weather. During "the long winter," Laura and her family read the old issues slowly to make them last until the next delivery.

Magazines such as The Youth's Companion *helped to cheer the long, cold nights on the prairies. These magazines, like most goods at the time, were moved to and around the Middle West by railroad. Turn the page to find a song about one of the country's best-known railroads.*

THE WABASH CANNONBALL

by A. P. Carter

In the mid-1900s, the Wabash Cannonball was one of America's best-known trains. The name "Wabash" comes from the Wabash River in the Middle West. Why do you think they called the train the "Cannonball"?

Music by William Kindt
Words adapted by Merrill Stanton

1. From the waves of the At - lan - tic to the wild Pa - ci - fic shore,
Refrain Now___ lis - ten to her rum - ble, now___ lis - ten to her roar,

From the coast of Cal - i - for - nia to snow - bound La - bra - dor,
As she ech - oes down the val - ley and flies a - long the shore.

There's a train of fan - cy lay - out that's well known to us all,
Now___ hear the en - gine whis - tle, It's a might - y lone - some call.

It's the ho - bo's home when he wants to roam ___ It's the Wa - bash Can - non - ball.
As we ride the bars and the emp - ty cars ___ on the Wa - bash Can - non - ball.

2. There's lots of places, partner, that you can go to see.
   St. Paul and Kansas City, Des Moines and Kankakee,
   From the lakes of Minnehaha where the laughing waters fall,
   You reach them by no other than the Wabash Cannonball. *Refrain*

3. For years I've ridden on this line across the countryside.
   I've always been well treated, tho' I took the hobo's ride.
   And when my days are over, and the curtains 'round me fall,
   Please ship me off to Heaven on the Wabash Cannonball. *Refrain*

DOTY'S WASHER

Advertising Poster from the 1800s

In the late 1800s, technology was advancing in leaps and bounds in the United States. Between 1860 and 1900, the first automobiles, telephones, telegraphs, electric lamps, and radios were produced. Cameras and sewing machines, invented in the early 1800s, became popular. People were urged to buy all kinds of wonderful new machines. The advertising poster below shows a washing machine of the 1800s—"Doty's Clothes Washer" with the new "Universal Clothes Wringer." In what ways do you think a new machine like the "Doty's Clothes Washer" changed the lives of women?

THE PAST.   THE PRESENT.

HOUSEKEEPERS, TAKE YOUR CHOICE.

DOTY'S CLOTHES WASHER, lately much improved, and the new UNIVERSAL CLOTHES WRINGER, with Rowell's Expansion Gear, and the patent "Stop," save their cost twice a year by saving clothes, besides shortening the time and lessening the labor of washing nearly one-half.

A FAIR OFFER.—Send the retail price:—WASHER, $14; EXTRA COG-WHEEL WRINGER, $9—and we will forward to places where no one is selling, either or both, free of charges. If, after a trial of one month, you are not entirely satisfied, we will REFUND THE MONEY on the return of the machines, FREIGHT FREE.   R. C. BROWNING, General Agent,
Large Discount to the Trade everywhere.   32 Cortlandt St., New York.

Family Farm

by Thomas Locker

Life on a small farm is a lot of work. It means hours of chores for everyone. But even though farm families work very hard, it can still be difficult to make enough money. This story tells about one family's year on a small dairy farm. The two children, Mike and Sarah, have just found out some bad news. What problems does the family face? How will they keep the farm going?

None of my friends sit with their sisters on the school bus, and neither do I. But the day we heard that our school was going to be closed, I did.

"Sarah, you said they'd never close down our school!"

"Leave me alone, Mike," she said, and she stared out the window.

"Why couldn't they close the school in Warren instead, and make those kids ride to our school? I don't want to sit on a bus for three hours every day! How are we supposed to have enough time to do our chores?"

"How should I know, Mike?" Sarah answered. "I guess we'll just have to get up earlier."

As soon as we got home, Sarah went looking for Mom. She was out in the garden, gathering the best pumpkins for tomorrow's trip to the market. Sarah told her the terrible news.

Dad and Grandpa had driven to town to deliver the last load of our corn crop, so I just started in on my own chores.

Before supper Sarah and I went out to the barn to work with our calf, Derinda. We groomed her and tried to lead her around on the **halter rope**. Then we tried to get her to drink milk from the pail.

halter rope: rope used for leading an animal

"Come on, Derinda," Sarah said, "you're too old to be drinking from that big baby bottle."

"She'll never win a ribbon at the fair if she doesn't start growing soon," I said.

Then we heard the brakes on our grain truck squeal as Dad and Grandpa pulled up.

"Suppertime!" Mom called.

Dad and Grandpa were really quiet at supper. When I told them about our school closing, Grandpa just said, "With so many folks giving up and moving away, we'll be lucky if there are enough children left to fill the Warren school."

"You can't blame the farmers," Dad said. "The money we got from our corn crop today hardly covered the cost of seed, and gas for the tractor. And the price you get for milk these days is still way too low." He glared at Grandpa, then added, "If we had bought that land last year, maybe we could have raised enough to stay in farming."

"If we had bought that **overpriced** land, we would be **bankrupt** by now!" Grandpa snapped.

"Now, Pop, please don't start that again!" Mom said. "Things have got to get better." She turned to Dad. "Honey, do you think you could find a job to see us through until it's time for spring planting?" she asked.

"Maybe," Dad said.

That night I was so worried, I couldn't sleep. I saw a light on in Sarah's room, so I tiptoed past Mom and Dad's room and tapped quietly on Sarah's door. "Come in, Mike," she whispered.

"Sarah, if we lose the farm, what will happen to the animals? Where would we go? Would we have to move to the city?"

Sarah shook her head slowly and said, "We can't! What about Grandpa? He's lived his whole life on this farm."

Mom must have heard us. Opening the door, she said, "It's late, and you both should be asleep. Remember, tomorrow is Saturday, and we're taking a load of pumpkins to town. And don't worry," she added gently, "Somehow we'll find a way to keep the farm going. We always have."

A few years ago, when the bills started to pile up, we had to borrow from the bank to keep the farm going. Mom had wanted to get a job at the restaurant in town, to help out, but Dad didn't want her to do that. So last spring Mom planted a big garden of flowers, and pumpkins to sell at Halloween.

After morning milking we loaded the cool, slippery pumpkins in the pickup truck and drove to town. Nearly everyone wanted our pumpkins! "I can't believe it!" I told Mom and Sarah. "We sold every one!"

"And the florist asked us to bring more flowers," Sarah added.

overpriced: costing too much
bankrupt: out of money

When we got home, Dad said, "Pumpkins sure sell better than corn!"

"Then why don't we plant pumpkins?" Sarah asked.

Dad shrugged. "Selling a few pumpkins is one thing, but how would we sell thousands of them?"

A few weeks later my uncle Charlie, who is a **foreman** at the electric switch factory, helped Dad get a job. Our family was lucky because there weren't many jobs around.

On Dad's first day on the job I set my alarm to ring at five o'clock, an hour earlier than usual. Sarah and I would have to help Mom and Grandpa do the morning chores that Dad usually did.

Sarah is a sleepyhead. She hates to get up in the morning. "Wake up, Sarah," I called.

"Go away! It's still dark!"

But finally she got up, and we went out into the pasture and brought in the cows. Grandpa turned the radio on to the **gospel music** station, as he always did, and he and Dad started milking.

When they were finished, I got a pail of milk for the barn cats. Just before he left for work, Dad called to us: "Thanks, kids! See you tonight."

It was tough keeping the farm running with Dad away all day. Grandpa cleaned the barn after milking, and he hardly ever went into town to drink coffee at the café with the other **retired** farmers. He worked all day. Sarah quit the volleyball team so we could both come home right after school. I decided not to try out for the basketball team this year. We took care of the calves and fed the pigs. The days were growing shorter and the sun was down when Dad got back for the evening milking.

Winter came. The old furnace at school wasn't working well, and some days it was really cold in our classroom. So the school boards decided that instead of getting a new furnace, we should start going to the Warren school right after Christmas vacation.

Changing schools didn't turn out to be so bad. It was fun meeting all the new kids from Warren. The gym was much newer, and everyone said that we would have a great basketball team. And the bus ride wasn't really that much longer.

One evening before supper Sarah and I were out in the barn feeding the calves. Derinda was finally growing, but we hadn't

foreman: person in charge of a group of workers, especially in a factory

gospel music: church music

retired: no longer working

had much time to work with her.

"If we don't start getting Derinda to lead on the halter, she won't have a chance to win a ribbon at the fair," I told Sarah.

"I know," Sarah said, "but there just isn't enough time. It'll be great when spring comes and Dad can work full-time on the farm again."

But in February things started to get even worse. First Grandpa hurt his back and couldn't work. Our neighbors helped, but it was Mom who kept things going.

Corn prices were still low. Dad said it wouldn't pay to plant a crop, and he'd have to keep on working at the factory.

But things were slow at the factory, and we heard **rumors** that they might start **laying off** workers. If that happened, Dad said we'd have to sell the farm and move to the city, where he could find work.

rumors: stories without facts to support them

laying off: firing

Mom cried a lot and said, "We can't just give up!"

Then Sarah got a great idea. We decided to wait for just the right time to tell Dad.

The spring **thaw** began, and one warm Sunday morning we decided to walk to church. On the way back Sarah asked, "Dad, if we can't earn enough from corn this year, why don't we plant flowers and pumpkins? Mike and I could set up a farm stand by the main road and sell them to all the people that drive by."

thaw: weather warm enough to melt ice and snow

Grandpa said, "You know, I've been thinking about pumpkins. A few fields might just make the difference for a farm like ours. But we might have to sell some of them to the food stores."

"We didn't have any trouble selling everything from the garden last fall," Mom said.

"We'd have to sell an awful lot of pumpkins to make a go of it. Do you really think we could do it?"

"I think so," said Grandpa.

"I'm a dairy farmer," said Dad. "I don't know anything about flowers or pumpkins."

"We can learn," Mom said.

We talked and talked. Then, when Dad got laid off at the factory, that did it! We decided to give it a try. We planted enough hay, oats, and corn to feed our animals through the winter, and the rest we planted in pumpkins and flowers.

By June the first seeding of flowers were in bloom, but so were the weeds. I couldn't believe how much work it took to raise flowers. We had to weed by hand, and spray and feed those plants all the time.

"If we were trying to grow weeds instead of flowers," Sarah said, "we'd be rich!"

When summer vacation came, we had a lot more time. But Sarah was never around—she and Grandpa were always driving somewhere to deliver truckloads of flowers—so I had to try to train Derinda by myself.

That summer my legs had finally gotten long enough to reach the clutch pedal on the old tractor. Dad started to teach me how to drive.

As we drove past the flower patch I saw that some of the flowers were **withering**. "Dad, a lot of the flowers are spoiling in the field. I know we're selling some, but do we earn enough to pay for the gas it takes to **haul** them?"

withering: drying up

haul: carry

"Don't worry, Mike," he told me. "We've made some money on the flowers and now we know a lot of store owners who will sell our pumpkins at Halloween time. You know, we might just do all right."

Summer ended, and except for thousands of bright orange pumpkins, the color faded from the fields. Dad and Grandpa went back to all the stores that had bought our flowers and delivered tons of pumpkins. Sarah and I set up the roadside stand, and by Thanksgiving most of the pumpkins were gone! Dad and Grandpa even started talking about renting some land to plant a crop of Christmas trees.

We took Derinda to the fair, but when it was our turn to lead her past the judges, she **balked** and kicked. It was lucky I had a good grip on the rope. She didn't win anything, and we brought her home and put her with the rest of the dairy herd.

balked: stopped short

We were disappointed, of course. But a few days later, as we were closing the pasture gate, Dad called to Sarah and me, "Come to the barn. I have something for you."

There, nestled in the straw, was a beautiful newborn calf, who could win a ribbon at next year's county fair!

Everyone in the family worked extra hard to keep the farm going. But no one really minded because the farm was more important to them than anything else. Farm families often have to work together. Have you ever had to work hard for something you wanted? How did it make you feel?

Source: Thomas Locker, *Family Farm*. New York: Dial, 1988.

Working the Land

by Pierce Walker

In 1972 the writer Studs Terkel interviewed Pierce Walker, an Indiana farmer. When he was a boy, Pierce Walker lived on a farm of 80 acres. As an adult, he had a farm of 250 acres, and he worked an additional 250 acres for other people. How did Pierce Walker feel about the technology—that is, the new machines— that he used to farm his land?

Farming, it's such a gamble. The weather and the prices, and everything that goes with it. You don't have too many good days. It scares you when you see how many working days you actually have. You have so many days to get the crop planted and the same in the fall to harvest it. They have this all figured down to the weather. It tenses you up. Whether we needed rain or we didn't need rain, it affects you in different ways. I have seen a time when you're glad to hear the thunder and lightning. Then again, I've wished I didn't hear it. (Laughs). . .

Weather will make ya or break ya. The crops have to have enough moisture. If they don't have enough, they hurt. If you have too much, it hurts. You take it like you git. There's nothing you can do about it. You just don't think too much about it. My wife says it doesn't bother me too much. Of course, you still worry. . . .

I don't believe farmers have as much ulcers as business people 'cause their life isn't quite as fast. But I'll say there will be more as time goes on. 'Cause farming is changing more. It's more a business now. It's getting to be a big business. It's not the labor any more, it's the management end of it.

Your day doesn't end. A farmer can't do like, say, a doctor— go out of town for the weekend. He has to stay with it. That's just one of the things you have to learn to live with. I'd say a majority of the time a farmer, when he comes in at night and goes to bed, he's tired enough he's not gonna have trouble sleepin'. Of course, he'll get wore down. . . .

My father-in-law helps me an awful lot in the spring and a little in the fall. He drives the tractor for me. My daughter, she drives a tractor when school is out. When I was home there on the farm, there were five children, three boys, and we were on an eighty-acre farm. It took all of us, my father and three boys. You can see the difference machinery plays in it.

The number of farmers is getting less every day and just seems like it's getting worse every year. The younger ones aren't taking over. The majority of the people **originated** from the farm years ago. But it's been so long ago that the young ones now don't realize anything about the farm. What goes with it or anything like that. The **gamble** that the farmer takes.

originated: started

gamble: risk

The city people, when they go to the grocery store and the price of meat is raised, they jump up and down. They don't realize what all is behind that. They're thinking of their own self. They don't want to put up that extra money—which I don't blame them either. The same way when I go to buy a piece of equipment. I go jump up and down. . . .

When you get a good crop, that's more or less your reward. If you weren't proud of your work, you wouldn't have a place on the farm. 'Cause you don't work by the hour. And you put in a lot of hours, I tell you. You wouldn't stay out here 'til dark and after if you were punchin' a clock. If you didn't like your work and have pride in it, you wouldn't do that.

You're driving a tractor all day long, you don't talk to anyone. You think over a lot of things in your mind, good and bad. You're thinking of a new piece of equipment or renting more land or buying or how you're going to get through the day. I can spend all day in the field by myself and I've never been lonesome. Sometimes I think it's nice to get out by yourself. . . .

This interview comes from a collection of interviews by Studs Terkel. Terkel wanted to know how all different kinds of Americans felt about their jobs, so he traveled around America asking them and tape-recording their answers. Whom would you like to interview about his or her job?

Source: Studs Terkel, *Working*. New York: Random House, Inc., 1972.

THE SOUTHWEST

*I am a pueblo child and I love
to listen to my grandparents
tell stories.*

from *Pueblo Storyteller*
by Diane Hoyt-Goldsmith

The ERRAND

by Harry Behn

In Harry Behn's poem, "The Errand," a boy in the Southwest returns a book for his father to a neighboring farmer. His journey turns out to be very special for him. What does the boy see on his journey that is typical of the geography of the Southwest region?

I rode my pony one summer day
Out to a farm far away
Where not one of the boys I knew
Had ever wandered before to play,
Up to a tank on top of a hill
That drips into a trough a spill
That when my pony drinks it dry
Its trickling takes all day to fill;
On to a windmill a little below
That brings up rusty water slow,
Squeaking and pumping only when
A lazy breeze decides to blow;
Then past a graveyard overgrown
with gourds and grass, where every stone

Leans crookedly against the sun,
Where I had never gone alone.
Down a valley I could see
Far away, one house and one tree
And a flat green pasture out to the sky,
Just as I knew the farm would be!
I was taking a book my father sent
Back to the friendly farmer who lent
It to him, but who wasn't there;
I left it inside, and away I went!
Nothing happened. The sun set,
The moon came slowly up, and yet
When I was home at last, I knew
I'd been on an errand I'd never forget.

Why do you think the poet will never forget the errand he did that day? What errands have you done that you will never forget?

Source: Harry Behn, *The Golden Hive*. New York: Harcourt, Brace, 1966.

I'm in Charge of Celebrations

by Byrd Baylor

To some people, the desert is a lonely place. To others, it is a land of magical surprises. For the young girl in Byrd Baylor's poem "I'm in Charge of Celebrations," the desert is a place where marvelous things happen. Why does she celebrate the New Year in the spring? How does she know when spring has come to the desert?

Friend,
I've saved
my New Year Celebration
until last.

Mine
is a little
different
from the one
most people have.

It comes in
spring.

To tell the truth,
I never did
feel like
my new year
started
January first.

To me,
that's just
another
winter day.

I let my year
begin
when winter
ends
and morning light
comes
earlier,
the way it *should.*

That's when
I feel like
starting
new.

I wait
until
the white-winged doves
are back from Mexico,
and wildflowers
cover the hills,
and my favorite
cactus
blooms.

107

It always
makes me think
I ought to bloom
myself.

And
that's when
I start to plan
my New Year
celebration.

I finally choose
a day
that is
exactly
right.

Even the air
has to be
perfect,
and the dirt
has to feel
good and warm
on bare feet.

(Usually,
it's a Saturday
around the end
of April.)

I have a drum
that I beat
to signal
The Day.

Then I go
wandering off,
following all
of my favorite
trails
to all of the
places
I like.

I check how
everything
is doing.

I spend the day
admiring
things.

If the old desert tortoise
I know from last year
is out
strolling around,
I'll go his direction
awhile.

I celebrate
with horned toads
and ravens
and lizards
and quail. . . .
And, Friend,
it's not
a bad
party.

In other parts of this poem, the poet celebrates different desert events: the day the whirlwinds blew, the day a triple rainbow appeared in the sky, and the day that she met a coyote. If you were "in charge of celebrations" where you live, what special events would you choose to celebrate?

Source: Byrd Baylor, *I'm in Charge of Celebrations*. New York: Charles Scribner's Sons, 1986.

PUEBLO STORYTELLER

by Diane Hoyt-Goldsmith

April Trujillo is a ten-year-old Pueblo girl who lives in a small town near Santa Fe, New Mexico. In the book, Pueblo Storyteller, *April describes one of the many Pueblo traditions she has learned. What traditions have you learned from your family?*

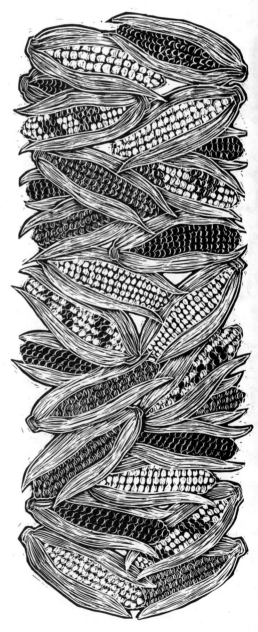

For me there is a special time at the end of the day. After the work is finished and I am ready to go to bed, my grandmother and grandfather tell me stories from the past. Sometimes they tell about the legends of the pueblo people. Other times they tell about things that happened in their own lives.

My grandmother likes to tell about when she was a girl. She lived in a Tewa (tay' *wah*) pueblo to the north called San Juan. She remembers autumn, a time when her whole family worked together to harvest and husk the corn crop. The corn came in many colors—red and orange, yellow and white, blue and purple, and even the deepest black.

Her family would sit in the shade of a ramada (rah-mah'-dah) built of cedar branches. Sheltered from the hot sun, the workers would remove the husks from a mountain of colorful corn. All the time they were working, they would laugh at jokes, sing songs, and share stories.

My grandmother tells me there were always lots of children around—her brothers and sisters, their cousins and friends—and they always had fun. My grandfather tells how the boys would use their slingshots to hurl stones at the crows who came too close to the corncobs that were drying in the sun.

When I was very young, my grandparents told me a legend about how our ancestors found the place where we are living today, our pueblo along the Rio Grande River. They call it "How the People Came to Earth," and it is still one of my favorite tales.

How the People Came to Earth

Long, long ago, our people wandered from place to place across the universe. Their leader was Long Sash, the star that we call Orion. He was the great warrior of the skies. Long Sash told his people that he had heard of a land far away, a place where they could make a home.

Because the people were weary of wandering, they decided to follow Long Sash on the dangerous journey across the sky to search for a new home. They traveled on the Endless Trail, the river of countless stars that we call the Milky Way.

The way was hard for our people. Long Sash taught them to hunt for food, and to make clothing from the skins of animals and the feathers of birds. Even so, they were often hungry and cold, and many died along the way. Long Sash led them farther than any people had ever gone before.

After a time, the people came to a vast darkness, and they were afraid. But Long Sash, the great warrior, believed they were heading the right way, and led them on. Suddenly, they heard the faint sound of scratching. Then, as they watched, a tiny speck of light appeared in the distance. As they got nearer, the light grew larger and larger. Then they saw that it was a small hole leading to another world.

When they looked through the opening, they saw a little mole digging away in the earth. Long Sash thanked the mole for helping them to find their way out of the darkness. But the mole only replied, "Come in to our world. And when you see the sign of my footprints again, you will know you have found your true home." The people saw a cord hanging down from the hole and they all climbed up and went through into the new world.

My grandparents are storytellers who have brought the past alive for me through their memories, through their language, through their art, and even through the food we eat. I am thankful that they have given me this rich history. From them I have learned to bake bread in an ancient way, to work with the earth's gift of clay, and to dance to the music of the Cochiti drums.

I am a pueblo child and I love to listen to my grandparents tell stories. From their example, I learn to take what I need from the earth to live, but also how to leave

Once through the opening, Long Sash saw Old Spider Woman busily weaving her web. He asked permission to pass through her house. Old Spider Woman replied, "You may come through my house. But when you next see the sign of my spiderweb, you will have found your true home."

The people did not understand what Old Spider Woman meant, but they thanked her and continued on their journey.

Long Sash and his followers traveled to many places on the earth. They found lands of ice and snow, lands where the sun burned and the air was dry, and beautiful lands with tall trees and plenty of game for hunting. In all of these places, they searched for signs of the mole and Old Spider Woman, but found nothing.

Some of the people stayed behind in the lands they discovered, but Long Sash and most of the tribe kept going. They kept searching for their true home.

Finally they came to a new land where the seasons were wet and dry, hot and cold, with good soil and bad. They found, here and there, small tracks that looked like a mole's. They followed the tracks and found a strange-looking creature, with ugly, wrinkled skin. The slow-moving animal carried a rounded shell on its back.

Long Sash was very happy when he saw the creature. "Look!" he said. "He carries his home with him, as we have done these many years. He travels slowly, just like us. On his shell are the markings of the spiderweb and his tracks look just like the mole's."

When our people saw the turtle, they knew they had found the homeland they had traveled the universe to discover. And we still live on those same lands today.

something behind for future generations. Every day I am learning to live in harmony with the world. And every day, I am collecting memories of my life to share one day with my own children and grandchildren.

Perhaps there is someone who reads to you or tells you stories. Do you like hearing stories? Why is storytelling different from watching television or going to a movie?

Source: Diane Hoyt-Goldsmith: *Pueblo Storyteller*. New York: Holiday House, 1991.

An American Cowboy Song

Many people think that "dogies" are dogs—but "dogies" is the name cowboys used for the motherless calves that strayed from the herds on the long drives from Texas to the railroads. When the cowboys drove their herds north, they sang to themselves and to each other. Sometimes, as in this song, the cowboys sang to the dogies! How does the music sound like cattle moving along?

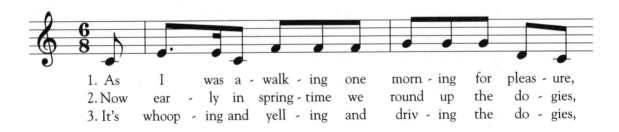

1. As I was a - walk - ing one morn - ing for pleas - ure,
2. Now ear - ly in spring - time we round up the do - gies,
3. It's whoop - ing and yell - ing and driv - ing the do - gies,

I spied a cow - punch - er a - rid - ing a - long;
We mark them and brand them and bob off their tails;
Oh, how I wish you_____ would go right a - long;

His hat was thrown back and his spurs were a - jing - lin',
We drive up our hors - es and load the chuck wag - on,
It's whoop - ing and punch - ing, git on, lit - tle do - gies,

And as he ap - proached he was sing - ing this song.
Then throw_____ the do - gies out on - to the trail.
You know that Wy - o - ming will be your new home.

Refrain

Whoop-ee ti - yi - yo, git a - long, lit - tle do - gies,

It's your mis - for - tune and now of my own;

Whoop-ee ti - yi - yo, git a - long, lit - tle do - gies,

You know that Wy - o - ming will be your new home.

Kate Heads West

by Pat Brisson

In Pat Brisson's story, Kate Heads West, *Kate is invited to join her best friend Lucy on her family's vacation. Lucy's family is going to tour the Southwest by car. Kate and Lucy learn a lot about the Southwest and have a great time. You can learn about their trip by reading some of the postcards Kate sends back to her friends and family in New Jersey. Which places would you want to visit if you were a tourist in the Southwest?*

August 6, Fort Worth, Texas
Dear Buster and Bruno,

I hope Brian's keeping your bowl nice and clean like he promised he would. If he threatens to flush you down the toilet, tell him I won't give him the **genuine** cowboy hat I bought for him at the rodeo last night in Fort Worth.

My favorite part of the rodeo was the cowgirls racing their horses around barrels in big figure eights. They went around the corners so fast it looked like the horses would fall right over. Lucy and I would probably be world champion barrel-racers if we lived in Texas and owned horses.

Yesterday afternoon we went to a Japanese garden. It was very quiet and peaceful there. Lucy's mom told us the Meditation Garden is just like one she's been to at a temple in Kyoto, Japan. She said it's nice to find a little bit of Japan in Texas. And there were beautiful **imperial carp** swimming in the pools there which reminded me of you.

Your favorite owner,
Kate

P.S. Tell Mom and Dad not to worry—I'm being really polite.

imperial carp: a kind of fish that lives in ponds, like a goldfish

114

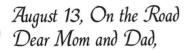

August 13, On the Road
Dear Mom and Dad,

We're on the longest drive of the vacation—480 miles from San Antonio to Carlsbad, New Mexico.

Lucy and I sang "The Stars at Night Are Big and Bright, Deep in the Heart of Texas" for the first 100 miles. But then Mrs. T. asked us to do something quiet like count cactus plants. We only got up to sixty-seven.

Then Lucy's dad said we should stop and stretch our legs. Opening the car door was like opening an oven door. My face started baking as soon as I got out. But the air smelled beautiful, not quite like flowers but just as nice.

I thought the desert would be completely empty except for sand. But there are lots of plants, and I saw some birds (but no roadrunners), and two rabbits with the longest ears I've ever seen, and four lizards and some bugs. I was hoping we'd see a **scorpion** or a **tarantula**, but we weren't that lucky.

scorpion: a small poisonous animal
tarantula: a poisonous spider

Your favorite daughter,
Kate

P.S. Hey, Brian, remember Davy Crockett and the battle at the Alamo? We went there yesterday. It looked a lot bigger on TV.

August 17, El Paso, Texas
Buenos Días, Aunt Mag (that's Spanish for "good day"),

I'm on vacation in Texas with my friend Lucy and guess what—we *walked* to Mexico yesterday! (We walked from El Paso across the Rio Grande to Juarez.) It was my first time in another country and it was great! I spent the money you gave me on a beautiful skirt, which comes down to my feet, and a blouse with little flowers embroidered all over it. *Muchas gracias!* (That means "thank you very much.")

Your favorite niece,
Kate

P.S. Here's some more Spanish that I learned: *Dispensame* means "excuse me" and *yo quiero a Mexico!* means "I love Mexico!"

August 18, Buckhorn, New Mexico
Dear Mrs. Heath,

How are things at the library? We visited the Gila Cliff Dwellings National Monument today. We had to climb a narrow trail to get there, and one spot was perfect for hearing your echo from the opposite wall of the canyon. Lucy and I yelled our names to see how many echoes we could get back. (Lucy got six, but I got seven.)

Anyway, the cliff dwellings are stone buildings built right into the side of the cliff. They are about a thousand years old! The Mogollon Indians built them for protection from other tribes. I guess it worked, because they lived here for hundreds of years.

Your favorite reader,
Kate

August 23, the Petrified Forest, Arizona
Dear Brian,

We are having the *best* time! Today we went to the **Petrified** Forest. It wasn't like I expected, but it was still great. I thought there would be all these trees standing around looking like concrete. But there aren't that many trees at all and actually, they're lying around like logs. They look like marbles all melted together—swirls of red and yellow and purple and pink.

I took some great pictures of the petroglyphs (old rock carvings made by the Anasazi Indians). My favorite is a mountain lion with his claws bared and his mouth open in a terrible snarl.

Tomorrow we're going to see the Hopi Snake Dance. Mr. T. said the Hopi dance with live rattlesnakes in their mouths without getting bit. We are also going to visit a pueblo built on a mesa. Mesas are hills with steep sides and flat tops, almost like tables.

Aren't you glad you're my little brother? There's so much you can learn from me.

Your favorite sister,
Kate

petrified: changed into stone

116

August 28, Grand Canyon, Arizona
Dear Mom and Dad,

Thank you, thank you, thank you for letting me come on this trip with Lucy! I can't believe I'll be home in less than a week. We're spending these last days at the Grand Canyon before we fly back. I think they should have named it the Stupendously Gigantic Canyon because it is so unbelievably big. In some places the river is a *mile* down from where we stand—I've even seen birds flying below me. At one lookout point we looked down and saw clouds. Lucy said it was fog, but I think it's the same thing.

We learned so much here that the park ranger gave us Official Junior Ranger Badges!

Yesterday we went river rafting in another canyon. Lucy and I screamed almost the entire trip, and Mr. T. said he had to give our guide a really big tip because we probably broke his eardrums.

Your favorite daughter,
Kate

When Kate returned home at the end of the trip, she had many more stories to tell, about the land, the history, and the people of the Southwest. What are some things Kate and Lucy learned about on their trip? Have you ever taken a trip to a different region of the country?

Source: Pat Brisson, *Kate Heads West*. New York: Bradbury Press, 1990.

THE TEXAS SPIRIT

by Barbara Jordan

Barbara Jordan was elected to the United States House of Representatives from Texas in 1972. Her victory was very unusual at the time because very few women were representatives. It was also very unusual because Jordan is African American. Texas had never before elected an African-American woman to serve in the House of Representatives. Jordan left the House of Representatives in 1979. Since then, she has continued to work hard to create more opportunities for all people. In 1989 Brian Lanker interviewed Barbara Jordan for his book, I Dream a World. How does Jordan's life reflect the spirit of Texas that she describes in her interview?

When I was a student at Texas Southern University in Houston, I had to ride the bus from my house to school across town. There was a little **plaque** on the bus near the back that said **"Colored"** and when I'd get on I'd have to go all the way back to that little plaque and I was passing empty seats all the time.

plaque: sign
colored: old word for African Americans

In 1962, I lost a contest for the state House of Representatives. And some of the people were saying that I probably lost the race because people are just not **accustomed to** voting for a woman. And I just said, "Well, now, that is totally ridiculous and I'll just have to try to alter that."

accustomed to: used to

All my growth and development led me to believe that if you really do the right thing, and if you play by the rules, and if you got enough good, solid judgment and common sense, that you're going to be able to do whatever you want to do with your life. My father taught me that.

The civil rights movement called [upon] America to put a giant mirror before it and look at itself. I believe that the movement said to America, "Look at what you have been saying to us black people all of these years. Look what you have been trying to sell us as the bill of goods for America. Look at that and then ask yourselves, have you really done it? Do the black people who were born on this soil, who are American citizens, do they really feel this is the land of opportunity, the land of the free, the home of the brave, all that great stuff?"

And when America looked into that giant mirror and heard these questions, the drumbeat—that's what the movement was, this drumbeat of questions—America had to say, "No, I really haven't, as a country, lived up to what I've said this country could be for you." And so the civil rights movement was a time of requiring that America be honest in its promises. And that was the goodness of the movement.

I am telling the young people that if you're dissatisfied— and I don't think they can be students in a school of public affairs and not be dissatisfied—if you are dissatisfied with the way things are, then you have got to **resolve** to change them. I am telling them to get out of there and occupy these positions in government and make the decisions, do the job and make it work for you. . . .

resolve: decide

Texas is more than a place. It is a frame of mind. A Texan believes that the individual is powerful. Texas has that rugged individualism. It may not be polished, may not be smooth, and it may not be silky, but it is there. I believe that I get from the soil and the spirit of Texas the feeling that I, as an individual, can accomplish whatever I want to and that there are no limits, that you can just keep going, just keep soaring. I like that spirit.

Since 1979 Barbara Jordan has been a professor at the University of Texas in Austin. What experiences in her life do you think she could teach about to others? Why do you think teaching can be as important as serving in the United States House of Representatives?

Source: Brian Lanker, *I Dream a World*. New York: Stewart, Tabori & Chang, 1989.

JUSTIN AND THE BEST BISCUITS IN THE WORLD

by Mildred Pitts Walter

Ranchers today use modern machines and modern methods in their work, but in some ways they are like the cowboys of the Southwest 100 years ago! In Mildred Pitts Walter's novel, Justin and the Best Biscuits in the World, *10-year-old Justin goes to visit his grandfather's ranch. Justin is excited to leave his family behind for the visit. He thinks his sister and his mother always make him do "girl's work." Now he thinks he'll get to learn about real "man's work," ranch work. What are some of the unexpected things that Justin learns about cowboys of the past and work on ranches today?*

The sun beamed down and sweat rolled off Justin as he rode on with Grandpa, looking for broken wires in the fence. They were well away from the house, on the far side of the ranch. Flies buzzed around the horses and now **gnats** swarmed in clouds just above their heads. The prairie resounded with songs of the bluebirds, the **bobwhite quails**, and the

gnats: small insects
bobwhite quails: birds that sing "Bob white! Bob white!"

mockingbirds **mimicking** them all. The cardinal's song, as lovely as any, included a whistle. . . .

mimicking: imitating

It was well past noon and Justin was hungry. Soon they came upon a small, well-built shed, securely locked. Nearby was a small stream. Grandpa reined in his horse. When he and Justin **dismounted**, they hitched the horses, and unsaddled them.

dismounted: got off their horses

"We'll have our lunch here," Grandpa said. Justin was surprised when Grandpa took black iron pots, other cooking **utensils**, and a table from the shed. Justin helped him remove some iron rods that Grandpa carefully placed over a shallow pit. These would hold the pots. Now Justin understood why Grandpa had brought uncooked food. They were going to cook outside.

utensils: tools

First they collected twigs and cow **dung**. Grandpa called it cowchips. "These," Grandpa said, holding up a dried brown pad, "make the best fuel. Gather them up."

dung: manure

There were plenty of chips left from the cattle that had fed there in winter. Soon they had a hot fire.

Justin watched as Grandpa carefully washed his hands and then began to cook their lunch.

"When I was a boy about your age, I used to go with my father on short runs with cattle. We'd bring them down from the high country onto the plains."

"Did you stay out all night?"

"Sometimes. And that was the time I liked most. The cook often made for supper what I am going to make for lunch."

Grandpa put raisins into a pot with a little water and placed them over the fire. Justin was surprised when Grandpa put flour in a separate pan. He used his fist to make a hole right in the middle of the flour. In that hole he placed some shortening. Then he added water. With his long delicate fingers he mixed the flour, water, and shortening until he had a nice round mound of dough.

Soon smooth circles of biscuits sat in an iron skillet with a lid on top. Grandpa put the skillet on the fire with some of the red-hot chips scattered over the lid.

Justin was amazed. How could only those ingredients make good bread? But he said nothing as Grandpa put the chunks of smoked pork in a skillet and started them cooking. Soon the smell was so delicious, Justin could hardly wait.

Finally Grandpa suggested that Justin take the horses to drink at the stream. "Keep your eyes open and don't step on any snakes."

Justin knew that diamondback rattlers sometimes lurked around. They were dangerous. He must be careful. He watered Black first.

While watering Pal, he heard rustling in the grass. His heart pounded. He heard the noise again. He wanted to run, but was too afraid. He looked around carefully. There were two black eyes staring at him. He tried to pull Pal away from the water, but Pal refused to stop drinking. Then Justin saw the animal. It had a long tail like a rat's. But it was as big as a cat. Then he saw something crawling on its back. They were little babies, hanging on as the animal ran.

A *mama opossum and her babies*, he thought, and was no longer afraid.

By the time the horses were watered, lunch was ready. "M-mmm-m," Justin said as he reached for a plate. The biscuits were golden brown, yet fluffy inside. And the sizzing pork was now crisp. Never had he eaten stewed raisins before.

"Grandpa, I didn't know you could cook like this," Justin said when he had tasted the food. "I didn't know men could cook so good."

"Why, Justin, some of the best cooks in the world are men."

The look he gave Grandpa **revealed** his doubts.

revealed: showed

"It's true," Grandpa said. "All the cooks on the cattle trail were men. In hotels and restaurants they call them chefs."

"How did you make these biscuits?"

"That's a secret. One day I'll let you make some."

"Were you a cowboy, Grandpa?"

"I'm still a cowboy."

"No, you're not."

"Yes, I am. I work with cattle, so I'm a cowboy."

"You know what I mean. The kind who rides bulls, **broncobusters**. That kind of cowboy."

broncobusters: cowboys who tame horses

"No, I'm not that kind. But I know some."

"Are they famous?"

"No, but I did meet a real famous Black cowboy once. When I was eight years old, my grandpa took me to meet his friend Bill Pickett. Bill Pickett was an old man then. He had a ranch in Oklahoma."

"Were there lots of Black cowboys?"

"Yes. Lots of them. They were hard workers, too. They busted **broncos**, branded calves, and drove cattle. My grandpa tamed wild **mustangs**."

broncos: wild horses
mustangs: horses

"Bet they were famous."

"Oh, no. Some were. Bill Pickett created the sport of **bulldogging**. You'll see that at the rodeo. One cowboy named Williams taught Rough Rider Teddy Roosevelt how to break horses; and another one named Clay taught Will Rogers, the comedian, the art of roping." Grandpa offered Justin the last biscuit.

bulldogging: wrestling with bulls that have long, sharp horns

When they had finished their lunch they led the horses away from the shed to graze. As they watched the horses, Grandpa went on, "Now, there were some more very famous Black cowboys. Jessie Stahl. They say he was the best rider of wild horses in the West."

"How could he be? Nobody ever heard about him. I didn't."

"Oh, there're lots of famous Blacks you never hear or read about. You ever hear about Deadwood Dick?"

Justin laughed. "No."

"There's another one. His real name was Nat Love. He could outride, outshoot anyone. In Deadwood City in the Dakota Territory, he roped, tied, saddled, mounted, and rode a wild horse faster than anyone. Then in the shooting match, he hit the bull's-eye every time. The people named him Deadwood Dick right on the spot. Enough about cowboys, now. While the horses graze, let's clean up here and get back to our men's work . . ."

As they cleaned the utensils and dishes, Justin asked, "Grandpa, you think housework is women's work?"

"Do you?" Grandpa asked quickly.

"I asked you first, Grandpa."

"I guess asking you that before I answer is unfair. No, I don't. Do you?"

"Well, it seems easier for them," Justin said as he splashed water all over, glad he was outside.

"Easier than for me?"

"Well, not for you, I guess, but for me, yeah."

"Could it be because you don't know how?"

"You mean like making the bed and folding the clothes."

"Yes." Grandpa stopped and looked at Justin. "Making the bed is easy now, isn't it? All work is that way. It doesn't matter who does the work, man or woman, when it needs to be done. What matters is that we try to learn how to do it the best we can in the most enjoyable way."

"I don't think I'll ever like housework," Justin said, drying a big iron pot.

"It's like any other kind of work. The better you do it, the easier it becomes, and we seem not to mind doing things that are easy."

With the cooking rods and all the utensils put away, they locked the shed and went for their horses.

"Now, I'm going to let you do the **cinches** again. You'll like that."

cinches: the straps that fasten the saddles on to the horses

There's that teasing again, Justin thought. "Yeah. That's a man's work," he said, and mounted Black.

"There are some good horsewomen. You'll see them at the rodeo." Grandpa mounted Pal. They went on their way, riding along silently, scanning the fence.

Finally Justin said, "I was just kidding, Grandpa." Then without planning to, he said, "I bet you don't like boys who cry like babies."

"Do I know any boys who cry like babies?"

"Aw, Grandpa, you saw me crying."

"Oh, I didn't think you were crying like a baby. In your room, you mean? We all cry sometime."

"You? Cry, Grandpa?"

"Sure."

They rode on, with Grandpa marking his map. Justin remained quiet, wondering what could make a man like Grandpa cry.

As if knowing Justin's thoughts, Grandpa said, "I remember crying when you were born."

"Why? Didn't you want me?"

"Oh, yes. You were the most beautiful baby. But, you see, your grandma, Beth, had just died. When I held you I was flooded with joy. Then I thought, *Grandma will never see this beautiful boy*. I cried."

The horses wading through the grass made the only sound in the silence. Then Grandpa said, "There's an old saying, son. 'The brave hide their fears, but share their tears.' Tears bathe the soul."

Justin looked at his grandpa. Their eyes caught. A warmth spread over Justin and he lowered his eyes. He wished he could tell his grandpa all he felt, how much he loved him.

Over the summer, Justin learns a lot about ranching from his grandfather. At the end of the summer, Justin wins a prize at the rodeo. He returns home to his family proudly—with ribbons, a new cowboy hat, and the ability to bake "the best biscuits in the world!" Justin's grandfather teaches him many different kinds of things. In the selection that you have just read, which "lesson" do you think is the most important?

Source: Mildred Pitts Walter, *Justin and the Best Biscuits in the World*. New York: Lothrop, Lee & Shepard Books, 1986.

BILL PICKETT

Cowboy Movie Poster

In Justin and the Best Biscuits, Justin's grandfather tells him about Nat Love and other African-American cowboys. The most famous rodeo cowboy of all was Bill Pickett. Pickett was half African American and half Chocktaw Indian. He was known for roping cattle, riding broncos, and bull-dogging. Pickett could jump on top of a bull, grab its horns, and wrestle it to the ground. What does this movie poster tell you about Bill Pickett?

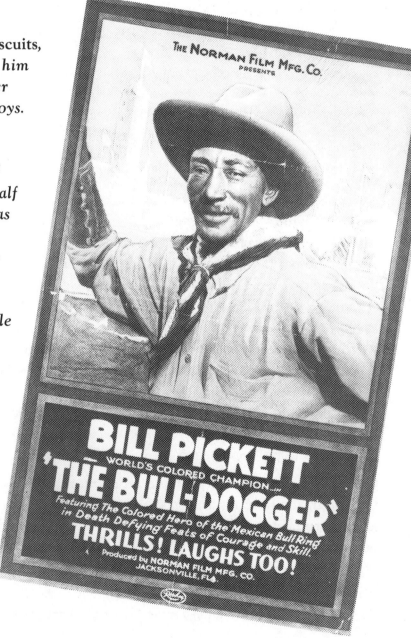

An Apache Girl Becomes a Woman

by Telly Declay

Almost 1 million Native Americans live in the United States today. Some live in cities and towns with people of many different backgrounds. Others live on reservations with people of their own groups. Many Native Americans practice traditions that are hundreds of years old. Telly Declay, a 12-year-old White Mountain Apache girl who lives in the Southwest, wrote a magazine article describing a traditional ceremony in which she was going to take part, with the help of her family and tribe. This ceremony is called the Sunrise Dance, which is held for Apache girls to mark their passage into womanhood. Why is this ceremony important to Telly?

My name is Telly. I am Apache and I'm 12 years old. I'm from the White Mountain Reservation in Arizona. I live in the town of Whiteriver. It's a long way to the nearest big city. Phoenix is about 5 hours away by car. The roads are steep and kind of dangerous where they wind through the mountains. . . .

I'll be in Junior High this year. I'm looking forward to the dances and football games. I am even trying out for cheerleader.

My school will be putting on a Christmas play. I want to try out for a part.

My favorite school subject is computer science because my dad sells computers. He showed me how to use them. My dad's also a contractor. He builds things. He helped to build the hospital and elementary school here in Whiteriver. He even built the house we live in.

My mom is a fire fighter. She had to train a long time to learn how to fight forest fires. It's hard work and it can be very dangerous. You have to be strong. When there is a fire, she has to work very long hours. She gets dirty and hot. She puts her life in danger in order to save others and to save the forests. Mom is proud of the work she does.

Something very, very important is going to happen to me in two weeks. I'm having my Sunrise Dance. It lasts for four days. It's the biggest ceremony of the White Mountain Apache Tribe. It's performed when an Apache girl passes from childhood into womanhood. My mother never had a Sunrise Dance so she is excited about mine. She explained how important it is. She told me, "Then you will live to an old age. You will be strong during your life."

My parents have spent a year getting ready for the ceremony. They asked our relatives to help them. A medicine man helped choose my **sponsors**. The sponsors have to be an older couple who are not related to us. I will call them my godparents. My mother and father will take an eagle feather to the home of my godmother. They will place it on her foot and ask her to prepare a dance for me. When she picks it up, she has answered, "Yes."

sponsors: people who help and support

Mother told me what will happen at my Sunrise Ceremony. The first night my godmother will pin an eagle feather on my head. This will help me live until my hair turns gray. She will fasten an **abalone** shell in my hair so that it lies on my forehead. This is the sign of Changing Woman, mother of all Apache people. During the whole ceremony godmother will massage my body. She is giving me all her knowledge through her hands. That night the crown dancer will dance around the fire. I will follow him because he **represents** spirits who protect us.

abalone: a sea snail that has a pretty shell

represents: symbolizes, stands for

The second day is Saturday and it's going to be hard. It's like an **endurance** test. The men begin to chant at dawn. The chant is really a prayer. I have to kneel on a **buckskin** pad and move my body like I'm dancing. I face the sun, who is the

endurance: strength and patience
buckskin: deer skin

Creator. After I have done this, I must run around a sacred cane and prove my strength. My godmother and other women in my family will run behind me. My dress will be made of buckskin and it will be heavy. Mother says I won't even notice. My spirit will carry the **burden**.

On Sunday, the third day, my godfather will direct my dancing. He will take an eagle feather in each hand. My father will stand next to him holding my sacred cane. When I am a very old woman, I will use this cane to help me walk. The handle of the cane is decorated with the feathers of the oriole. The oriole is a sweet-tempered bird. It will help me to be sweet-tempered, too.

On both Saturday and Sunday, I am showered with bright yellow powder. This is the pollen of the cattail. It is holy to my people. We use it as a blessing. Perhaps as many as a hundred people will walk by me. Each one will take a handful of pollen and shake it over my head. Each person will say a silent prayer for me. In return, I will pray to the sun, asking for blessings on all those people who are sharing this special time with me.

Next, my father pours candies and kernels of corn over me. This will protect me from hunger in my life. Then my whole family passes out gifts to the guests. This means we hope that the people will *always* have plenty to eat.

The number Four is the most important number to Apache people. There are four seasons and four directions. It is a sacred number. On Sunday, Godfather paints me with a mixture made from pollen, cornmeal, and ground-up stones of four colors. He paints me from the top of my head to the bottom

burden: heavy load

129

of my buckskin boots. This means I am protected from all four sides. Later on, the paint will dry and brush off my outfit. I will be able to wear the outfit at any Apache dance. I am proud of my outfit because many people helped to make it. My Aunt Linda sewed the buckskin top. Another aunt cut and rolled about 200 small pieces of tin into little cones. When they are sewn on the dress, they will jingle. It will make me sound like wind in the trees when I walk. My Aunt Zoe made my velvet camp dress.

Mother says that for four days, I won't be able to take a bath, touch my skin, or drink from a glass. Godmother has made a string that will attach to the neck of my dress. A cloth and a tube will be tied to the string. The cloth will be used to wipe my face. I will drink from the tube. It's made from reeds.

The men from the tribe will build a tepee frame. I must dance through it several times on Sunday so that the spirits will always make sure I have a home. Late in the day my mother will follow me through the tepee for the last time. When darkness comes, the dancing will be done.

On Monday morning many people will come to visit me and offer their blessings. Aunt Zoe will be proud if I don't cry. In the Apache tribe, the people in the mother's **clan** are very important. Aunt Zoe is my mother's sister and I will listen carefully to what she tells me. I want to make her proud. By the end of the fourth day, I will be a young woman instead of a little girl.

clan: family group

When we say "thank you" to Godmother, we'll do it in a big way. We will have a feast. All our relatives have made dozens of dresses, quilts and blankets. These will be given away to our guests. It takes a lot of hard work and a long time to pay back all the people who have come to my Sunrise Dance.

I'm really glad my family is able to have a Sunrise Dance for me. Not all Apache families can afford it or still believe it's important. But it's part of our tradition. My parents care for me. They want me to grow up in the right way. The Sunrise Dance is the right way for Apache girls.

Many cultures and religions have ceremonies for young people to welcome them into young manhood or young womanhood. What ceremonies do you know of that celebrate the beginning of becoming an adult?

Source: Telly Declay, "Our Life Today. . .As White Mountain Apaches." *Daybreak Star*: Seattle, Washington, November 1987.

6

THE WEST

Ten-year-old Hector Almaraz is a Mexican American. For as long as he can remember he has lived in Los Angeles—in this neighborhood, on this block.

from *Hector Lives in the United States Now* by Joan Hewett

SIERRA

by Diane Siebert

In her poem, "Sierra," Dianne Siebert traces the history of the Sierra Nevada mountains. She begins with their birth millions of years ago, and then describes how they changed over the years to become what they are today: a beautiful site with a great variety of plant and animal life. What are some of the plants and animals that live in the Sierra Nevada mountains today?

I am the mountain,
    Tall and grand.
And like a **sentinel** I stand.   **sentinel:** guard
Surrounding me, my sisters rise
With watchful peaks that **pierce** the skies;   **pierce:** cut
From north to south we form a chain
Dividing desert, field, and plain.
    I am the mountain.
      Come and know
Of how, ten millions years ago,
Great forces, moving plates of earth,
Brought, to an ancient land, rebirth;
Of how this planet's **faulted crust**   **faulted:** cracked or
Was shifted, lifted, tilted, thrust   broken, resulting in
Toward the sky in waves of change   earthquakes
To form a newborn mountain range.   **crust:** top layer of the
    I am the mountain,   earth
      Young, yet old.

I've stood, and watching time unfold,
Have known the age of ice and snow
And felt the **glaciers** come and go.

glaciers: huge sheets
of ice

They moved with every melt and freeze;
They shattered boulders, leveled trees,
And carved, upon my granite rocks,
The terraced walls of **slabs** and blocks

slabs: big, flat pieces
of rock

That trace each path, each downward course,
Where through the years, with crushing force,
The glaciers sculpted deep **ravines**

ravines: valleys

And polished rocks to glossy sheens.
At last this era, long and cold,
Began to lose its **frigid** hold

frigid: icy

When, matched against a warming sun,
Its final glacier, ton by ton,
Retreated, melting, making way
For what I have become today:
A place of strength and **lofty** height;

lofty: very high

Of shadows shot with shafts of light;
Where meadows nestle in between
The arms of forests, cool and green;
Where, out of **clefted** granite walls,

clefted: creased

Spill silver, snow-fed waterfalls.
Here stand the pines, so straight and tall,
Whose needles, dry and dying, fall
Upon my sides to slowly form
A natural blanket, soft and warm;
Their graceful, swaying branches sing
In gentle breezes, whispering
To junipers, all **gnarled** and low,

gnarled: knotted

That here, in stubborn splendor, grow.
And on my western slope I hold
My great **sequoias**, tall and old;

sequoias: tallest trees
in the world

They've watched three thousand years go by,
And, in their endless **quest** for sky,

quest: search

This grove of giants slowly grew
With songs of green on silent blue.

I am the mountain.
In each breath
I feel the pull of life and death
As untamed birds and beasts obey
The laws of **predator** and **prey**.

predator: an animal
that hunts other
animals

prey: animals hunted
by predators

On me, the hunted ones reside,
Sustained by foods my plants provide:
I keep the **pikas**, small and shy,
That spread their gathered grass to dry.
I shelter rodents. In my trees
Live pinecone-loving **chickarees**,
While tunnels, **crevices**, and holes
Hold **marmots**, ground squirrels,
   chipmunks, **voles**.
I cradle herds of graceful deer
That drink from waters cold and clear;
I know each **buck** with antlers spread
Above his proud, uplifted head.
I know each doe, each spotted fawn,
In sunshine seen, in shadows, gone.
I know these creatures, every one.
They, to survive, must hide or run;
As food for those that stalk and chase,
Within life's chain, they have a place.
Then, too, the predators are mine,
Each woven into earth's design.
I feel them as they wake and rise;
I see the hunger in their eyes.
These are the coyotes, swift and lean;
The bobcats, shadowy, unseen;
The **martens** in their tree-branch trails;
The masked raccoons with long, ringed tails;
The mountain lions and big black bears
That live within my rocky **lairs**;
The owls that prowl the skies at night;
The hawks and eagles, free in flight.
I know them all. I understand.
They keep the balance on the land.
They take the old, the sick, the weak;
And as they move, their actions speak
In tones untouched by right or wrong:
        We hunt to live.
        We, too, belong.
    I am the mountain.
        From the sea
Come constant winds to conquer me—
Pacific winds that touch my face

pikas: small rodents similar to rabbits

chickarees: red squirrels

crevices: narrow openings

marmots: mountain mice

voles: a kind of rodent

buck: male deer

martens: animals like weasels

lairs: dens

And bring the storms whose clouds embrace
My rugged shoulders, strong and wide;
And in their path, I cannot hide.
And though I have the strength of youth,
I sense each change and know the truth:
By wind and weather, day by day,
I will, in time, be worn away;
For mountains live, and mountains die.
As ages pass, so, too, will I.
But while my cloak of life exists,
I'll **cherish** winds and storms and mists,
For in them, precious gifts are found
As currents carry scent and sound;
As every gust and playful breeze
Helps **sow** the seeds of parent trees;
As silver drops and soft white flakes
Fill laughing streams and alpine lakes;
As lightning fires, hot and bright,
Thin undergrowth, allowing light
To reach the fresh, cleared soil below
So roots can spread and trees can grow.
          I am the mountain,
            Tall and grand,
        And like a sentinel I stand.
Yet I, in nature's wonders **draped**,
Now see this mantle being shaped
By something new—a force so real
That every part of me can feel
Its actions changing nature's plan.
Its numbers grow. Its name is MAN.
And what my course of life will be
Depends on how man cares for me.
          I am the mountain,
            Tall and grand.
        And like a sentinel I stand.

cherish: love and treasure

sow: spread, scatter

draped: dressed

Diane Siebert says that "MAN" is a new force whose actions change nature's plans. What does she mean by this? She says that the life of the Sierra Nevada mountains depends on how man cares for them. How do you think that people can take care of mountains?

Source: Diane Siebert, *Sierra*. New York: HarperCollins, 1991.

ROLL ON, COLUMBIA

by Woody Guthrie

There are many songs that describe the beauty of this country's rivers, but this is one of the few that describes how we use our rivers for electric power. In the late 1930s, many people in this country did not have electricity. The United States government started a program that helped bring hydroelectric power to the western United States. Woody Guthrie, a famous folk singer, wrote this song to celebrate the Columbia River. What does Guthrie mean when he says, "Your power is turning our darkness to dawn"?

Words by Woody Guthrie

Music based on "Goodnight Irene" by Huddie Ledbetter and John Lomax

1. Green Doug - las fir where the wa - ters cut through,
2. Oth - er big riv-ers add_____ pow - er to you,

Down her wild moun - tains and can - yons she flew.
Yak - i - ma, Snake, and the Klick - i - tat, too.

136

Ca - na - di - an North - west to the o - cean so blue,
__ Sand - y, Wil - lam - ette, and the Hood Riv - er, too,

Roll on, Co - lum - bia, roll on._____

Refrain

Roll on,___ Co - lum - bia, roll on. Roll on,___ Co-

lum - bia, roll on. Your pow - er is turn - ing our

dark - ness to dawn, Roll on, Co - lum - bia, roll on.___

Source: Woody Guthrie, *Roll On, Columbia*. New York: Ludlow Music, Inc. 1936.

ARCTIC MEMORIES

by Normee Ekoomiak

Even in summer, when flowers bloom in the Arctic, there is a layer of ice lying beneath the ground that is frozen forever. The Inuit have learned to live with this cold. Many of their stories tell about surviving in a world of snow and ice. In his book Arctic Memories, *writer and artist Normee Ekoomiak remembers growing up on Hudson Bay in Canada in the 1950s. Hudson Bay is a region that is very similar to northern Alaska. Although today few Inuit people live in igloos made of snow, Normee Ekoomiak's family did when he was a little boy. How did his family get food during the long arctic winters?*

In the Iglu

"**Iglu**" means house. When I was small, we used to live in a snow house in the winter and in a tent the rest of the year. During the long winter up North, there is little sun and it is always dark. We stay inside and do our work and play.... When it starts to get warm, the snow house will melt. We will build a tent to live in, and we will move with it from place to place when we hunt for food. Inside the iglu there is an oil lamp on three legs. It is for light and for heat. But when we go to sleep, we put out the lamp, and then it gets cold, so we must all sleep together to keep warm. The kids sleep in the middle, between their parents.

iglu: another way to spell *igloo*

Okpik—The Lucky Charm

"Okpik" means "snowy owl." He is our friend, and his spirit protects all of nature in the North.... He is watching over a father who is going hunting with his dog and spear, and he is watching over a mother with a baby in the hood of her **amautig.** Okpik is also the **guardian** of the polar bear and of the geese. All of the nature spirits work together and watch over the North. We must keep them happy and only kill the right animals or else the spirits will not let us find food.

amautig: overcoat
guardian: protector

138

Ice Fishing

After a snowstorm it is hard to find caribou and seal and walrus. All of the birds and animals are gone. Sometimes months go by before they come back. So the whole family has to go out fishing, to catch the arctic **char**, through holes in the ice. **Sedna** is good, and she makes sure there are plenty of fish. But sometimes it is hard to catch any fish, and the birds and animals stay away for a long time. Then the people must move to a new camp if they are strong enough. Or else they will starve.

> **char:** a kind of fish, similar to trout
> **sedna:** the sea spirit

Hanging Fish

After the fish are caught, the people have to hang them up to dry and to freeze. They cannot leave the fish under the snow, or the polar bear or wolf or fox could find the fish and eat it. The snowy owl sees the polar bear coming and warns the people. They take the fish with them inside the iglus and wait for the bear to go away. Then they will hang the fish up again. Okpik watches over his people and makes sure their food is safe.

Arctic Spring

The ice is breaking up, getting ready to float across James Bay. It will soon be summer, and the Canada geese are flying north to lay eggs to make more Canada geese. If they are born in the South, they are not as healthy. There is too much pollution, and they do not have the right food. They like the North because it's natural for them. Nanook, the polar bear,

is hungry and looking for food. The mother seal calls the baby seal, and they swim away and are safe. Now the bear has to eat fish. He would like to eat seal, but if he eats too much of it, he will get wild. It is better for bears to eat fish most of the time. Then they can be our friends. . . .

Who I Am

I am an **Inuk**. I was born in a place of magic: at Cape Jones. This is where James Bay empties into Hudson Bay, on the east shore, the Quebec side. . . . I can remember everything. I grew up at Fort George in my grandfather's tent, which had a wooden frame and was covered in canvas and with seal skins. It was about ten feet by twenty feet. My grandfather taught me about Inuit ways and about how to do my art. My father and mother and six brothers and seven sisters lived with us. I went to school at the mission there. In 1971 I had to leave Fort George. I was too lonely. So first I went to Ottawa to stay with my sister and her family. I did my art and learned to eat some of the food of the South. Then in 1972 I came to George Brown College in Toronto and later went to the New School of Art. After that I made many paintings and drawings and wall hangings, which I sold to friends and to art galleries. I wanted to go back to Fort George, but the Hydro-Quebec James Bay Project has flooded the area and a new settlement called Chisasibi is now in the place where Fort George used to be. My North is not there any more. It is only in my memory.

Inuk: singular of Inuit; *Inuit* means "the people" and *Inuk* means "the person"

Today Normee Ekoomiak lives in a city in Canada, which he calls "the south." He lives in a modern building and eats food bought in the supermarket. How does Ekoomiak keep alive the traditions of his people?

Source: Normee Ekoomiak, *Arctic Memories*. New York: Henry Holt and Company, 1988.

When the Wind Blows Hard

by Denise Gosliner Orenstein

Today the Inuit live in all parts of Alaska. Although their way of life has changed over the last hundred years, many of their traditions remain. In the story below, Shawn's mother tells her that they will be leaving New York City and moving to Alaska. Shawn is miserable. "Alaska's at the end of the earth," she complains. When they arrive in the small town of Klawock, Shawn isn't any happier. Her classmates are all members of the Tlingit group and think her red hair is strange. Shawn in turn thinks her classmates seem strange. Soon, however, a Tlingit girl named Vesta becomes her best friend. In the selection below, Shawn makes another friend—Vesta's grandfather. Have you ever become friends with someone much older than you? How was the friendship special?

When I got to his house, I knocked on the door, waited for a minute, and then walked in. Vesta's grandfather was sitting at the table, just like before. He was cutting a piece of wood with a knife. Just like before. There was no reason to be nervous.

"Hello, young Shawn," he said.

"Hello," I said, setting his dinner down on the table. "I brought you something to eat. I thought you might like some more dinner tonight. This time, I made your dinner all by myself. My mother is at a teachers' meeting tonight."

Vesta's grandfather might have smiled just a little. It was hard to tell. He put one hand on my arm and pointed to a chair.

"Sit down," he said.

I sat down next to him. He picked up the piece of wood again and began cutting it with a knife. I had seen other men in Klawock cut wood like that. It's called carving. It's a kind of artwork. Vesta's grandfather began to talk as he carved. This is what he said:

"This wood is like the pulse of a wrist. It's full of motion and warm inside the hand. What I am carving is alive."

I watched the piece of wood change shape as he carved. It looked like magic. All at once, I could see the shape of a small, curved paddle.

"Are you carving a paddle?" I asked.

He nodded.

"This is a paddle like those from long ago. All we had to move our boats in those days were paddles. We had no engines. Even then, we carved our paddles like pieces of art. When I was small, like you, my uncle taught me to carve as I am carving now. My uncle was an artist and taught me not to do anything halfway. The Tlingit people treat art as something alive, something to be respected."

Vesta's grandfather had a way of speaking that really made you listen. Maybe it was because he spoke so softly. Maybe it was because he didn't speak often. Kind of like Vesta.

"Have you ever carved a totem pole?" I asked.

Vesta's grandfather nodded. "The totem pole in Klawock with the red fox on top, I carved that."

I couldn't believe it. The fox totem pole was my favorite. He continued talking.

"A person who makes totem poles has learned to study the animals. First, I had to study the fox. The fox is a lively creature and runs around like a small child. The fox is a symbol of a child."

He smiled and touched my hair.

"Your hair is red, like the color of the fox. You are lively and fast like the small animal the Tlingit people admire."

It was so nice to hear him say that. It made me feel warm.

"Did you paint the totem poles you carved?" I asked. "Totem poles are so big, so tall, how did you reach way up to paint them?"

Vesta's grandfather laughed.

"You paint the totems when they are lying down across the earth," he said, "before they are placed upright to stand in the sky. Long ago, we used paint brushes made from wild bushes and made all different kinds of paints from the nature around us. Some paints were made from tree bark, some from blueberries and blackberries. These old Indian paints last for hundreds of years. They never fade in the sun. Now, these paints from long ago are gone. Very few people remember them. But the totems remain."

"What do the other totem pole animals mean?" I asked. "Besides the fox totem?"

He was quiet for a moment.

"The crab is the symbol of the thief because he has so many hands. The mosquito represents teaching. When a mosquito bites, you start itching. Sometimes learning hurts."

He put the paddle down on the table next to the dinner I had brought and looked at me.

"This paddle is for you," he said. "Take it home. It will let you hear the sounds of long ago."

I felt funny. The paddle was so beautiful, but I didn't feel right taking the carving home. He picked up the paddle and handed it to me. It felt warm, warm from the heat of his hands.

"The Tlingit does not turn down any gift, " he said, "but accepts it with open arms."

That is when Vesta's grandfather and I finally became friends.

Walking home that evening I buttoned my jacket right up to my chin. It was getting colder; maybe the snow would be here soon. The cool air felt good on my cheeks and through the tangles of my red hair. A very thin frost—not quite ice, not quite snow—had covered the hill behind the school yard where the totem poles stood. I walked up the hill slowly, carefully, until I reached the top. The totem poles surrounded me in a large circle and I could hear the faraway hum of water brushing the shore. A quick wind blew hard and my ears stung a little from the cold, but I didn't put up my hood. I looked straight up at the totem poles and felt the small paddle in my jacket pocket. Something was shining in my heart.

A few months later, Shawn gets some sad news. Vesta and her parents are moving away from Klawock. Shawn thinks she'll never be happy there again. But after Vesta leaves, Shawn continues her friendship with Vesta's grandfather. She tells him, "You and I will . . . be each other's special family." After a while, she finds she doesn't miss New York City that much, and she loves Alaska, "even when the wind blows hard."

Source: Denise Gosliner Orenstein, *When the Wind Blows Hard*. Reading, Massachusetts: Addison-Wesley, 1982.

BY THE GREAT HORN SPOON!

by Sid Fleischman

Excitement ran high in the gold fields of California in 1849. People could have no money one day and be worth $ 1 million the next day if gold was discovered on their claim! But it didn't always work out that way. Sid Fleischman's novel By the Great Horn Spoon! *takes place during the California Gold Rush. It is a work of historical fiction. The characters are made up, but the historical details are true. In this section, 12-year-old Jack Flagg and Praiseworthy, the family butler, have just arrived in California. Their goal is to return to Boston with enough money to save the family home. What do they discover about life in the mining camps?*

There was road dust in Jack's eyebrows, in his ears and down his neck. Now that they had arrived he had gold fever so bad that he didn't see how he could wait another five minutes to get his shovel in the ground. . . .

It was exactly one hour and five minutes before Jack saw the **diggings**. First Praiseworthy registered at the hotel. They washed . . . "Can we go now?" said Jack, fidgeting. He had polished his **horn spoon** so much he could see his nose in it.

diggings: where the fortyniners panned for gold

horn spoon: a spoon made from a deer's antlers

"Go where?"

"The diggings."

"Oh, the diggings will still be there after lunch, Master Jack."

Praiseworthy's patience was a marvel—and an **exasperation.** They had come more than 15,000 miles and now they had to stop to eat. Jack didn't care if they passed up eating for a week. A month, even . . . .

"You and the boy want bread with your **grub?**" asked the waiter. He was a big fellow in floppy boots.

"Why not?" answered Praiseworthy.

"It's a dollar a slice."

The butler slowly arched an eyebrow.

"Two dollars with butter on it."

Praiseworthy peered at Jack, and then smiled. "Hang the cost, sir. We're celebrating our arrival. Bread and butter, if you please!"

The bear steak was greasy and stringy, but something to write home about. Jack forced it down. After they left the restaurant Praiseworthy bought a pair of buckskin pouches at the **general merchandise** store. . . . Jack liked the new leather smell of the pouch. He tucked it under his belt, next to the horn spoon, and was beginning to feel like a miner. Then, with tin **washbasins** under their arms and the pick and shovel across their shoulders, they set out for the diggings.

The day was hot and sweaty. When they reached running water they saw miners crouched everywhere along the banks. They were washing gold out of the dirt in everything from wooden bowls to frying pans.

"Anybody digging here?" asked Praiseworthy when they came to a bare spot.

"Shore is," came the answer. "That's Buffalo John's claim."

The butler and the boy moved on upstream . . . .

On and on they went, looking for a place to dig. They passed miners in blue shirts and red shirts and checked shirts and some in no shirts at all. Picks assaulted the earth and shovels flew. Weathered tents were staked to the hillsides and the smell of boiling coffee drifted through the air. After they had walked a mile and a half Jack began to think they would never find a patch of ground that wasn't spoken for.

Suddenly a pistol shot cracked the mountain air. Praiseworthy's washbasin rang like a bell and leaped from his arm and went clattering away.

exasperation: annoyance

grub: food

general merchandise: all kinds of things for sale

washbasin: washpan, a big bowl that could be used for washing your hands, your clothes, your plates—or panning for gold

"You there!" a voice from behind bellowed.

Praiseworthy turned. His eyes narrowed slowly. "Are you talking to me, sir?"

"Talkin' and shootin'. What you doin' with my washpan under your arm?"

Jack stared at the man. He had a thick, tangled beard and his ears were bent over under the weight of his slouch hat.

"Needless to say, you're mistaken," Praiseworthy answered. "Until this moment I've had the good fortune never to set eyes on you or your washpan, sir."

"We don't take kindly to thievery in these parts," growled the miner, stepping forward. "A man steals around here, we lop off his ears. That's miner's law."

"Do you have any laws against shooting at strangers?"

"Nope."

Jack couldn't imagine Praiseworthy with his ears lopped off. He took a grip on the handle of the shovel as the miner came closer. His heart beat a little faster and he waited for a signal from Praiseworthy.

The miner belted his pistol and picked up the washpan. He **crimped** an eye and looked it over.

crimped: squinted

"It's mine, all right."

"You're either near-sighted or a scoundrel," said Praiseworthy.

Jack was ready to fight, if not for their lives—at least for Praiseworthy's ears. Just then, a flash of tin in the sunlight, from a pile of wet rocks, caught Jack's eye. He dropped the shovel and went for it.

"Is this your pan?" Jack said.

The miner's bushy eyebrows shot up like birds taking wing. "It is at that, ain't it?" Then he laughed as if the joke were on him. "I'd forget my boots if I didn't have 'em on."

Praiseworthy peered at the man. Apparently, shooting at strangers by mistake didn't amount to anything in the diggings. The miner hardly gave it another thought.

Forty-Niners didn't usually include children and family servants. But in some ways Praiseworthy and Jack were typical fortyniners. They came to California to get rich quick and leave. And just like the other Forty-Niners, Jack and Praiseworthy realized it was not going to be nearly as easy as they had hoped.

Source: Sid Fleischman, *By the Great Horn Spoon!* Boston: Little, Brown and Company, 1963.

THE HEAVY PANTS OF MR. STRAUSS

by June Swanson

One of the unexpected results of the Gold Rush was blue jeans, which were created in California in the 1850s for gold miners. Levi Strauss made and sold hundreds and hundreds of these pants to the Forty-Niners, who needed strong clothing so that they could pan for gold. The Heavy Pants of Mr. Strauss is an essay by June Swanson that describes how blue jeans were invented during the Gold Rush. The advertisement shown on page 149 is from 1880, but is still used today. Early advertisements bragged that blue jeans were so strong that even two horses pulling in opposite directions couldn't pull the pants apart! Do you think this is why people buy blue jeans today?

On January 24, 1848, gold was discovered at Sutter's Mill in California. Almost overnight people were coming to California by the thousands, hoping to make a fortune in the new gold fields. In one year San Francisco grew from a small town to a city of 25,000 people. By 1850 the territory had a population of almost 100,000, and in that year California became the thirty-first state.

The new miners needed many things, and usually they had the money to buy whatever they wanted. This **abundance** of people with money to spend brought a great number of **peddlers** and merchants to California. One of these peddlers was a man named Levi Strauss.

abundance: great number

peddlers: traveling salesmen

In 1850 Levi Strauss made the long trip from the east coast to California by boat. The trip took him all the way around the southern tip of South America. With him, Levi Strauss brought yards and yards of heavy canvas to make tents for the miners and covers for their wagons.

However, when Strauss arrived in California, he found that the miners needed good, heavy pants much more than they needed tents. None of the pants available were tough enough to stand up against the rocks of the California hills and the hard

148

mining life. So Levi, seeing the possibility for a good business, made his tent canvas into pants instead of tents.

Strauss's tent canvas was a bit stiff for pants, so he began to make his pants out of a tough but less stiff material that he had sent to him from Nimes (Nēm), France. The material was called *serge de Nimes*. Serge is a kind of material, *de* means "from," and Nimes is the name of a city in France. Soon *serge* was dropped from the name, and the material was called *de Nimes*, or "denim."

The miners liked the denim pants so much that Levi couldn't make them fast enough. In fact, his pants were so well made that their basic design hasn't changed in over 100 years. Somewhere along the way they came to be called by their maker's first name—"Levi's."

Today the company that Levi Strauss began during the 1860s is still making the same basic straight-legged, button-fly, denim pants that he originally designed for the miners of California. Levi's have become so popular that they are sold (and copied) all over the world.

Blue jeans became very popular all over the United States. Today, they are made by many different companies and sold all around the world. Since Levi Strauss invented blue jeans in 1850, over 2 billion pairs of jeans have been sold.

Source: June Swanson, *The Spice of America*. Minneapolis: Carolrhoda Books, Inc., 1983.

Hector Lives in the United States Now

by Joan Hewett

The border between Mexico and the United States is 1,900 miles (3,057 km) long. Many people cross this border every day. People from Mexico often come to the United States in order to get work because there are more jobs available in the United States than in Mexico. In her book Hector Lives in the United States Now, *Joan Hewett writes about a real boy named Hector Almaraz, whose parents came to the United States to find work when Hector was a small boy. Hector and his parents were born in Mexico, but they have lived in Los Angeles, California, since Hector was about two years old. In what ways is Hector's life like yours? In what ways is it different?*

Ten-year-old Hector Almaraz is a Mexican American. For as long as he can remember he has lived in Los Angeles—in this neighborhood, on this block.

Hector's parents are Leopoldo and Rosario Almaraz. He also has three brothers: nine-year-old Polo, and Miguel and Ernesto, who are seven and four.

Hector and Polo were born in Guadalajara, Mexico, and are Mexican citizens, like their parents. Their younger brothers,

Miguel and Ernesto, were born in Los Angeles and are American citizens.

When Hector's parents came to California to find work, they did not understand English. But they had heard so much about Los Angeles, from sisters and brothers and their own parents, that the city seemed almost **familiar.**

At first they stayed with relatives. Then Leopoldo found a job, and the family moved to Eagle Rock, a **residential section** of the city.

They are still there. The streets and parks are safe, and an elementary school and a Catholic church are only a few blocks from their small, **bungalow-style** apartment.

Hector has lots of friends. Most of them live on this block. They play together after school and on Saturdays and Sundays.

Soccer is one of their favorite games. So is baseball. When it is baseball season, they dig out a bat, ball, and glove and practice batting in a backyard or alley. Other times they go to the park to play volleyball, or just to see what is going on. If no one has a flat, they ride their bikes over; otherwise they walk.

Like his friends, Hector likes to read comic books and collect baseball cards. Sometimes they gather their cards or books, meet on the front stoop, and trade. Although the children talk and joke in English, their parents come from Mexico and Central America, and Spanish is the language spoken in their homes.

When Hector and Polo are drawing or doing their homework at the kitchen table, they often tell stories to each other in English. They speak as fast as they can so their mother will not understand them. Rosario gets annoyed because she suspects they do it just to tease her.

Although Hector and Polo speak English equally well, their parents think it proper that their eldest boy be the family **spokesperson.** Hector enjoys the responsibility. Whenever someone who can only speak English telephones them, Hector is called to the phone. Or when Rosario has to get a **prescription** filled at the drugstore, Hector goes along to talk to the **pharmacist.**

Hector did not speak English when he started kindergarten. It was a scary time. He was away from his mother and brothers. He understood only a few English words and did not know

familiar: something you know

residential section: neighborhood where people live

bungalow-style: houses that are one-story high

spokesperson: person chosen to speak for the group

prescription: medicine order

pharmacist: druggist

what was going on in class. In first grade Hector had trouble learning to read. But he was **determined** to learn English, and by the end of the second grade he was reading and writing as well as his classmates. School started to be fun.

Now Hector is a fifth grader, one of the big kids. In United States history, his class is reading about the different immigrant groups who helped settle the West. Their teacher says, "We are a nation of immigrants. Indians, also called Native Americans, have lived here for thousands of years. Everyone else has come to the continental United States from some other place." Then she smiles and says, "Let's find out about us."

The students in Hector's class are told to ask their parents about their ancestors and then write a brief history of their families. It is an exciting project. When they finish their reports, they will glue snapshots of themselves to their papers and hang them on the wall. But first they get to read them aloud.

Philip traces his family back as far as his great-great-great-grandmother. His ancestors lived on a small Philippine island. Many of them were fishermen. Philip, his sister, and his parents are the only people in his family who have settled in the United States.

One side of Nicky's family came from Norway and Germany. His other ancestors came from Ireland and Sweden. All of them were farmers, and when they came to this country they homesteaded land, which means they farmed and built a house on **uncultivated** public land that then became theirs under a special homestead law.

Vanessa's great-great-grandmother was a Yaqui Indian from Sonora, Mexico. Her grandfather fought in the Mexican Revolution. Another one of her ancestors was French.

Erick is descended from Ukrainian, German, and Italian immigrants. His German grandfather and Ukrainian grandmother met in a prisoner-of-war camp. When they were released, they married and came to the United States by ship.

Julie is of French, Irish, and Spanish descent. Her Great-Great-Grandma Elm was born in Texas. When Elm was a child her family moved to California. They traveled by covered wagon.

Everyone is interested in Kyria's family history. One of her African ancestors was a soldier in the American Revolution. Another fought for the Confederacy in the Civil War. Other members of her family homesteaded in Oklahoma.

Hector tells the class about his Mexican ancestors. They were farmers and carpenters.

There are twelve other Mexican-American children in Hector's class, and some two hundred fifty thousand Mexican-American students in Los Angeles schools. . . .

Hector always tries to complete his homework during study period. When he can't, he finishes it at home. Hector's parents had only a grade school education, and his grandparents did not go to school at all. Hector knows that he is the first one in his family to have the chance to go on to high school, and he does not **intend** to let his family down.

intend: plan

Hector does not know yet what he wants to do after high school, but computers **intrigue** him, and he wonders if he might like working with them.

intrigue: interest

A few months ago he took a short beginner's computer lesson so that he could use the computers at his local public library. The library has computer games, and for a while he had great fun playing them. Then they seemed too simple. But he read a book about the different kinds of things computers can do and is looking forward to taking a real computer course when he's a little older.

Before Hector started using the library's computers he had only been to the library once, on a trip with his whole class. Now it is a place he visits regularly. Polo and Victor, one of his neighborhood friends, go with him. They take out books on building kites and drawing dinosaurs. And after watching TV dramas about John F. Kennedy, Robert Kennedy, and Martin

Luther King, Jr., Hector read books about them.

Because Hector is curious about past events and famous public figures, his parents gave him a thick, hardcover book about the last one hundred years of United States history. When no one is leafing through it, the book sits on a special shelf beside an English dictionary. Aside from the dictionary, it is the first English-language book Hector's family has purchased. . . .

One Saturday Leopoldo and Rosario announce that the whole family will be going to Guadalajara. Not this summer, because Leopoldo can't get off from work then. They will be going over Christmas vacation!

Hector is thrilled. He will see his grandparents and his aunts and uncles. He will be with Guadalupe, the cousin he has been writing to. His papa says they will take their van or go by bus. Either way, they will get to really see Mexico. And either way, he will get out of school two weeks early.

Leopoldo and Rosario talk about how happy they will be to see everyone. Starting Friday they will begin saving a little money each week so they can buy Christmas presents for everyone they will visit in Mexico. The boys want to know more about the trip.

Finally they run out of questions. Leopoldo leaves for the video store, taking Polo and Miguel with him. Rosario starts to make chili. Ernesto goes outside to play. And Hector and his friends head for the park.

In 1988 Hector and his parents applied for United States citizenship. It takes several years for people to become American citizens. Do you know anyone who was born in another country and now lives in the United States? Which country did they come from? Why did they come to the United States?

Source: Joan Hewett, *Hector Lives in the United States Now.* New York: J. B. Lippincott, 1990.

The Fun They Had

by Isaac Asimov

In California's "Silicon Valley" thousands of people make their living from the computer industry. Throughout the country today, computers have become a way of life. You might have a computer in your school, or even in your home. Not long ago, however, computers were very rare. The first computer, built in the early 1940s, was the size of an entire wall in your classroom. When Isaac Asimov wrote this story in 1957, computers were still used only by big companies and colleges. The story is science fiction and takes place in the future. Asimov imagined a time when computers would be used for everything. Do you think Isaac Asimov's imaginary future has come true?

Margie even wrote about it that night in her diary. On the page headed May 17, 2157, she wrote, "Today Tommy found a real book!"

It was a very old book. Margie's grandfather once said that when he was a little boy, his grandfather told him that there was a time when all stories were printed on paper.

They turned the pages, which were yellow and crinkly; and it was awfully funny to read words that stood still instead of moving the way they were supposed to—on a screen, you know. And then, when they turned back to the page before, it had the same words on it that it had had when they read it the first time.

"Gee," said Tommy, "what a waste. When you're through with the book, you just throw it away. I guess. Our television

screen must have had a million books on it, and it's good for plenty more. I wouldn't throw it away."

"Same with mine," said Margie. She was eleven and hadn't seen as many telebooks as Tommy had. He was thirteen.

She said, "Where did you find it?"

"In my house." He pointed without looking, because he was busy reading. "In the attic."

"What's it about?"

"School."

Margie was scornful. "School? What's there to write about school? I hate school."

Margie always hated school, but now she hated it more than ever. The **mechanical teacher** had been giving her test after test in geography, and she had been doing worse and worse until her mother had shaken her head **sorrowfully** and sent for the County Inspector.

mechanical teacher: robot

sorrowfully: sadly

He was a round little man with a red face and a whole box of tools with dials and wires. He smiled at Margie and gave her an apple, then took the teacher apart. Margie had hoped he wouldn't know how to put it together again, but he knew how all right; and, after an hour or so, there it was again, large and black and ugly, with a big screen on which all the lessons were shown and the questions were asked. That wasn't so bad. The part Margie hated most was the slot where she had to put homework and test papers. She always had to write them out in a punch code they made her learn when she was six years old, and the mechanical teacher **calculated** the mark in no time.

calculated: figured out

The Inspector had smiled after he was finished and patted Margie's head. He said to her mother, "It's not the little girl's fault, Mrs. Jones. I think the geography sector was geared a little too quick. Those things happen sometimes. I've slowed it up to an average ten-year level. Actually, the **overall** pattern of her progress is quite satisfactory." And he patted Margie's head again.

overall: total

Margie was disappointed. She had been hoping they would take the teacher away altogether. They had once taken Tommy's teacher away for nearly a month because the history sector had blanked out completely.

So she said to Tommy, "Why would anyone write about school?"

Tommy looked at her with very superior eyes. "Because it's not our kind of school, stupid. This is the old kind of school that they had hundreds and hundreds of years ago." He added **loftily, pronouncing** the word carefully, "Centuries ago."

loftily: proudly
pronouncing: speaking

Margie was hurt. "Well, I don't know what kind of school they had all that time ago." She read the book over his shoulder for a while, then said, "Anyway, they had a teacher."

"Sure they had a teacher, but it wasn't a regular teacher. It was a man."

"A man? How could a man be a teacher?"

"Well, he just told the boys and girls things and gave them homework and asked them questions."

"A man isn't smart enough."

"Sure he is. My father knows as much as my teacher."

"He can't. A man can't know as much as a teacher."

"He knows almost as much, **I betcha**."

I betcha: I bet you

Margie wasn't prepared to **dispute** that. She said, "I wouldn't want a strange man in my house to teach me."

dispute: argue

Tommy screamed with laughter. "You don't know much, Margie. The teachers didn't live in the house. They had a special building, and all the kids went there."

"And all the kids learned the same things?"

"Sure, if they were the same age."

"But my mother says a teacher has to be **adjusted** to fit the mind of each boy and girl it teaches, and that each kid has to be taught differently."

adjusted: have small changes made

"Just the same, they didn't do it that way then. If you don't like it, you don't have to read the book."

"I didn't say I didn't like it," Margie said quickly. She wanted to read about those funny schools.

They weren't even half-finished when Margie's mother called, "Margie! School!"

Margie looked up. "Not yet, Mamma."

"Now!" said Mrs. Jones. "And it's probably time for Tommy, too."

Margie said to Tommy, "Can I read the book some more with you after school?"

"Maybe," he said **nonchalantly**. He walked away whistling, the dusty old book tucked beneath his arm.

nonchalantly: calmly, cooly

Margie went into the schoolroom. It was right next to her bedroom, and the mechanical teacher was on and waiting for her. It was always on at the same time every day except Saturday and Sunday, because her mother said little girls learned better if they learned at regular hours.

The screen was lit up, and it said, "Today's arithmetic lesson is on the addition of proper fractions. Please insert yesterday's homework in the proper slot."

Margie did so with a sigh. She was thinking about the old schools they had when her grandfather's grandfather was a little boy. All the kids from the whole neighborhood came, laughing and shouting in the schoolyard, sitting together in the schoolroom, going together at the end of the day. They learned the same things, so they could help each other on the homework and talk about it.

And the teachers were people. . . .

The mechanical teacher was flashing on the screen, "When we add the fractions ½ and ¼ —"

Margie was thinking about how the kids must have loved it in the old days. She was thinking about the fun they had.

In Isaac Asimov's story, computers have taken the place of books and teachers and school. If you were to write a science fiction story about computers in the future, what tasks would they perform?

Source: Isaac Asimov, *The Earth Is Room Enough*. New York: Doubleday & Company, Inc., 1957.

The Alpine Song

Traditional Austrian Song

Yo De-Lay Hee-Hoo! Are those sounds familiar to you? Yodeling is a tradition in the mountains in Austria that has spread to other mountain areas around the world. Try it yourself with "The Alpine Song" below. When you see an asterisk (*), make the sound that follows it.

1. Oh, an Aus-trian went yo-del-ing on a moun-tain so high.
2. Oh, an Aus-trian went yo-del-ing on a moun-tain so high.

When a-long came an a-va-lance in-ter-rupt-ing his cry.
When a-long came a Saint Ber-nard in-ter-rupt-ing his cry.

Refrain

Yo-lay-dee, yo-de-lay-hee-hoo, Oh yo-de-lay-hee-hoo.

Yo-de-lay-hee-hoo, Oh yo-de-lay-hee-hoo. Yo-dee-lay-hee-hoo, Oh

yo-de-lay-hee-hoo. Yo-de-lay'-hee-hoo-oh lay.

1. * shh-shh . . .

2. * pant-pant . . .

3. Oh, an Austrian went yodeling on a mountain so high,
   When along came a Guernsey Cow interrupting his cry.
   * moo-moo, pant-pant, shh-shh.

4. Oh, an Austrian went yodeling on a mountain so high,
   When along came a Martian interrupting his cry.
   * beep-beep, moo-moo, pant-pant, shh-shh.

INDEX BY *Category*

Songs

Speeches and Interviews

TEACHING *Strategies*

Teachers share a common goal—to help their students become successful learners who can understand, remember, and apply important knowledge and skills. This important goal is best supported when students are offered a variety of ways in which to learn.

The Social Studies Anthology offers you precisely the rich and varied tools that you need to help your students learn. It includes such diverse sources as diaries, poems, songs, stories, legends, and posters—all of which draw children into the sights, sounds, and feelings of the places and times they are studying.

You may invite students to explore the Anthology selections in many unique ways—rewriting documents in another genre, dramatizing the selection, creating posters or collages, or writing original poems, stories, and songs. We have provided a strategy for teaching each selection in the Anthology. But these strategies, of course, are only suggestions. You should feel free to teach the selections in any way that you feel is best suited for your own classroom.

A Cassette and Activity Cards accompany the Social Studies Anthology and provide additional support in teaching the documents. A Cassette logo lets you know which selections have been recorded. Often, the recordings reproduce the voices of the people who actually wrote the selections. Activity cards can be used to link together the documents. They direct students in self-guided activities including hands-on projects and role playing.

SINCERELY, SAMANTHA
by Samantha Smith and Yuri Andropov
Pages 2–3

Use with Chapter 1, Lesson 1

Objectives

- ☐ *Explain Samantha Smith's motivation to write a letter to Yuri Andropov.*
- ☐ *Recognize that children such as Samantha Smith can make the world a better place for all of us.*
- ☐ *Write a letter to a foreign leader expressing concern for an issue.*

Background Information

In 1982, when Samantha Smith wrote her letter to Yuri Andropov, the Soviet Union and the United States were enemies. Since the end of World War II, relations between the two superpowers had been marked by a struggle for power. Mikhail Gorbachev, who became president of the Soviet Union in 1985, initiated reforms that eased the tensions between the two nations. During 1991 sudden changes in the government of the Soviet Union resulted in that nation's dissolution. The 15 republics that had formed the Soviet Union became independent nations. Russia and ten other former republics formed the Commonwealth of Independent States (CIS).

Writing Your Own Letter

After students have read the letters of Samantha Smith and Yuri Andropov, have them discuss the main concerns expressed by each writer. Ask students: *Why was Samantha motivated to write to the Soviet leader? What might Andropov have felt that prompted him to respond to Samantha's letter? How might the perspectives of people living in the United States and the former Soviet Union today have changed since 1982?*

Have students discuss problems that they know of in other countries. Then have each student write a letter to one of these country's leaders expressing his or her hope for a solution to the problems. After students have completed their letters, have volunteers read theirs to the class. Encourage students to mail their letters.

NO STAR NIGHTS
by Anna Egan Smucker
Pages 4–7

Use with Chapter 1, Lesson 2

Objectives

- ☐ *Identify the natural resources used for making steel.*
- ☐ *Recognize the beauty in the mill town described by Anna Smucker.*
- ☐ *Design a poster based on some of the descriptions of Weirton in No Star Nights.*

Creating Posters

After students have read the selection, discuss the various ways in which Anna Smucker describes life in a mill town. Discuss with students how the writer sees beauty in her harsh surroundings. Have students skim the story to find the vivid descriptions that Smucker uses to create images of Weirton. ("... turned the darkness into a red glow; golden spark-spitting steel; great puffy clouds of red, orange, and yellow")

Ask students to create a chart listing how the use of natural resources affected life in Weirton. Suggest that students skim the selection to find ways that the steel mill affected the environment. For example, great puffy clouds of red, orange, and yellow, but mostly the color of rust. Everything—houses, hedges, old cars—was a rusty red color. After students have completed the chart, display it on the bulletin board.

STATES AND CAPITALS
by Professor Rap
Pages 8–11 🔲

Use with Chapter 2, Lesson 1

Objectives

☐ *Recognize that our country is made up of 50 states, each of which is special.*

☐ *Recognize how Professor Rap uses rhyming words to help students to remember the names of state capitals.*

☐ *Write a rap song about your classroom or school.*

Writing Your Own Song

Play the song on the cassette for students and have them read along with the lyrics. Then ask volunteers to sing the song aloud. Students might enjoy singing the song in small groups.

Ask students to identify some of the words that rhyme with the names of state capitals. (*summery*, Montgomery; *snow*, Juneau; Honolulu, *ocean blue*; Tallahassee, *vitamin C*) Discuss the elements that make the song effective. (rhythm, rhyming words, refrain) Then have students work individually or in small groups to write a rap song about their classroom or their school.

Before students begin writing, have them brainstorm a list of rhyming words that they might use in their songs. Write the list on chart paper or on the chalkboard to help students get started. After students have completed their songs, have volunteers present them to the class. Students might enjoy making a recording of their songs.

A WALK ACROSS AMERICA
by Peter Jenkins
Pages 12–15

Use with Chapter 2, Lesson 1

Objectives

☐ *Identify the major landforms that are described in A Walk Across America.*

☐ *Recognize the enormous challenge that Peter Jenkins's walk across the country represented.*

☐ *Trace Peter Jenkins's route across the United States on a map.*

Tracing a Route

After students have read the selection by Peter Jenkins, direct their attention to the map in *Regions Near and Far* titled *United States Landforms* on pages 42–43. Remind students that the selection they have read described just one part of Jenkins's walk across the United States. Point out to students that the map shows the entire route taken by Peter Jenkins during his walk across America. Ask volunteers to name the different types of landforms found on Jenkins's route. (mountains, hills, plateaus, plains) Ask students which of these landforms were probably the most difficult for him to cross. (Mountains probably presented him with the most difficulty. Other types of landforms may have been just as difficult in bad weather conditions.) Ask students why much of Jenkins's route passed through the southern half of the United States. (Jenkins probably chose to take the southern route because weather conditions would be less harsh during the winter.)

As students trace Jenkins's route on the map, ask for volunteers to name each state that Jenkins traveled through. As students name the states, ask them to list the major landforms and cities that Jenkins passed through.

THIS IS MY ROCK

by David McCord
Page 16

Use with Chapter 2, Lesson 3

Objectives

- [ ] *Explain that David McCord uses poetry to describe what his rock means to him.*
- [ ] *Recognize that natural resources can be used in many ways.*
- [ ] *Write a poem about a natural resource.*

Writing Your Own Poem

After students have read the poem, ask volunteers to read it aloud to the class. Discuss with students why David McCord might have chosen to write a poem about a rock. Have volunteers tell about natural resources that are special to them. Encourage students to share examples, such as a favorite tree for climbing, a mountaintop, a meadow, a lake, a river, or a beach. Ask students: *In what ways are these natural resources special? Are they used or are they simply appreciated?* As students name examples, list them on chart paper or on the chalkboard.

Have each student write a poem about a natural resource of his or her choice. Encourage students to think about various times of the year when they might use or enjoy the resource they chose. After students have completed their poems, have them draw illustrations to accompany them. Encourage volunteers to share their poems and illustrations with the class.

50 SIMPLE THINGS KIDS CAN DO TO SAVE THE EARTH

by John Javna and The EarthWorks Group
Pages 17–20

TRASH—BUSTERS

from the *Kid City News*
Page 21

Use with Chapter 2, Lesson 3

Objectives

- [ ] *List ways in which people waste energy or contribute to pollution.*
- [ ] *Identify how we can improve the environment through recycling and conservation.*
- [ ] *Participate in activities to improve the environment.*

Building Citizenship

After students have read both selections, ask them to name the items mentioned that are important to recycle and conserve. Ask students: *Which of these items are recyclable?* (glass, plastic foam lunch trays) *Which of these items are not recyclable?* (Styrofoam products) *Which of these items are important to conserve?* (all)

Next have volunteers list ways in which they waste energy or contribute to pollution. Encourage them to suggest how they could waste less or conserve natural resources.

Divide the class into groups and have each group choose one conservation project—such as recycling glass, saving paper, or using less water. Have each group design a poster to publicize its project. Then have them display the posters in school hallways. If possible, have students carry out their projects—for example, students could set up recycling centers.

Students might enjoy referring to *50 Simple Things Kids Can Do to Save the Earth,* which is available in the Classroom Library.

SYMBOLS OF THE NATION
Pages 22–23

Use with Chapter 3, Lesson 3

Objectives

❏ *Explain how and why symbols are used to express ideas.*

❏ *Identify important symbols of the United States.*

❏ *Create symbols to represent your school or classroom.*

Creating Symbols

Have students read the selection and examine the symbols. Then ask them why people use symbols. (as a sign to represent something, to communicate without language) Ask volunteers to describe other national symbols not mentioned in the selection. (Possible examples include: Uncle Sam, the Lincoln Memorial, and the White House.)

Ask students to consider how they might use a symbol to represent their school or classroom. Have them work individually or in groups to design a symbol. Ask volunteers to write a brief description that explains their symbol. Then have them share their designs with the rest of the class. Display the symbols on the bulletin board.

BECOMING A CITIZEN
Pages 24–25

Use with Chapter 3, Lesson 1 and Traditions Lesson

Objectives

❏ *Describe the procedures that immigrants must follow in order to become citizens of the United States.*

❏ *Recognize some of the problems faced by immigrants coming to the United States.*

❏ *Write questions to ask in an interview with a recent immigrant to the United States.*

Writing an Interview

After students have read the selection, have them list some of the things that immigrants must do in order to obtain citizenship in the United States. (fill out application forms, take an oath of allegiance, interview with an Immigration and Naturalization Service official) Ask students: *What difficulties might new immigrants face as they apply for citizenship?* (problems with language, lack of money for fees) *Why are people willing to go through such a difficult process in order to acquire United States citizenship?* (Accept all reasonable answers.)

If possible, arrange to have a recent immigrant visit the class. Before the scheduled visit, have students work in pairs to write questions for the interview. Have one student in each pair write the question and have the other write the answer. After the interview, collect the questions and answers in a class book titled "Interviewing a New Immigrant." If possible, record the interview on a tape recorder.

NEW COLOSSUS
by Emma Lazarus
Page 26 [cassette icon]

Use with Chapter 3, Lesson 1

Objectives

☐ *Recognize some of the reasons that immigrants come to the United States.*

☐ *Identify how Emma Lazarus used poetry to describe the significance of the Statue of Liberty.*

☐ *Write a poem or short essay from the perspective of an immigrant arriving in New York Harbor.*

Rewriting from Another Perspective

After students have read the poem, play the recording on the cassette. Then ask a volunteer to read the poem aloud. Help students to understand difficult words or phrases.

Help students to understand that Emma Lazarus is presenting the statue's point of view in the lines, "Keep, ancient lands, your storied pomp!" The statue's point of view is continued in the line, "I lift my lamp beside the golden door!"

Have students imagine that they are immigrants arriving by ship in New York Harbor. Ask them how they might describe the Statue of Liberty and their feelings toward it. Then have students write their own poem or a brief essay from an immigrant's point of view. Have students illustrate their writing. Encourage volunteers to share their writings and illustrations with the class.

WALUM OLUM
by the Lenape-Algonquin People, 1700s
Pages 28–29

Use with Chapter 4, Lesson 1

Objectives

☐ *Understand that the Lenape-Algonquin handed down their creation story from generation to generation through storytelling.*

☐ *Recognize that during the 1700s the Lenape-Algonquin first wrote the Walum Olum in pictographs.*

☐ *Write a story using pictographs.*

Creating Your Own Pictographs

After students have read the selection and looked at the drawings, discuss why the Lenape-Algonquin used pictographs to write the Walum Olum. (They did not use an alphabet with letter symbols.) Ask students: *How do pictographs differ from other illustrations?* (Pictographs are simple line drawings.) Have students look closely at the pictographs to see if they can recognize what each symbol represents. Help students to recognize the sun, the crescent moon, the stars, and some of the animals in the pictographs.

Ask students to choose a familiar folktale that they know well—for example, Paul Bunyan, Johnny Appleseed, or Little Red Riding Hood. Discuss with students the characters and the story lines of several folktales. Then have students draw pictographs to represent the most important scenes in the story. Or students might choose to draw scenes from a story they make up themselves. Display the completed pictographs on the bulletin board.

SUGARING TIME
by Kathryn Lasky
Pages 30–33

Use with Chapter 4, Lesson 2

Objectives

❑ *Explain the steps for gathering and refining maple syrup as described in the selection.*

❑ *Describe the various uses for maple syrup.*

❑ *Draw a storyboard with captions for a video that explains sugaring time.*

Drawing Storyboards with Captions

After students have read the selection, have them discuss the methods used by the Lacey family to gather and refine maple syrup. (In March, when the sap begins to flow in the maple trees, tapholes are drilled into the trees and spouts are placed into the holes; buckets are hung on the spouts to collect the sap when it runs; the sap is taken to a storage house where it must be boiled within a week to prevent spoilage.) Ask students to name some ways to use maple syrup. (over pancakes, in maple candy, at sugar-on-snow parties)

Have small groups of students prepare storyboards for an imaginary video about how to make maple syrup. Ask each group of students to write a list of steps in the sugaring process. Then have them draw an illustration of each step. Finally, have them rewrite the list of steps to use as captions to explain the process clearly to potential viewers. After the storyboards have been completed, display them on the bulletin board.

THE LUMBERMAN'S ALPHABET
Pages 34–35

Use with Chapter 4, Lesson 2

Objectives

❑ *Recognize how the song "The Lumberman's Alphabet" reflects the daily life of the lumberjack.*

❑ *Identify how the lumberjacks used singing for socializing and entertainment.*

❑ *Write a song about school using the letters of the alphabet.*

Writing Your Own Song

After students have read the lyrics to the song, play it for them on the cassette. Ask volunteers to read the lyrics to the class.

Discuss with students why lumberjacks might make up songs. (to pass the time, to entertain themselves) Remind students that the lumberjacks worked deep in the forests where they spent many cold winter months. There were no towns or villages nearby to provide entertainment or relief from the hard work.

Have students rewrite "The Lumberman's Alphabet" with a new title, "The Student's Alphabet." Before students begin, have them brainstorm words for activities in school. For example, "A is for *Arithmetic*, and that we all know, and B is for *Books* that we read from to grow."

Divide the class into small groups and have each group write one verse. Encourage the class to write the chorus together. After the words to the song have been completed, make copies for everyone and have fun singing!

HARD TIMES AT VALLEY FORGE

by Joseph Martin, 1777–1778
Pages 36–37

Use with Chapter 5, Lesson 2

Objectives

- ☐ *Describe the hardships faced by the soldiers at Valley Forge as described in Joseph Martin's diary.*
- ☐ *Identify the reasons that Joseph Martin remained in the army despite the hardships.*

Rewriting in Another Genre

Have students share in reading this selection aloud. After the selection has been read, discuss with students the hardships described by Joseph Martin. (lack of food, water, clothing, and shelter; fatigue; freezing temperatures) Ask students which of Joseph Martin's experiences they consider to have been the most difficult. Have students look again at the selection to find a sentence in his diary that explains why Martin may have been willing to undergo such extreme hardship. (Martin wrote: "We had engaged in the defense of our injured country and were willing, nay, we were determined to persevere as long as such hardships were not altogether intolerable. . . .") Ask students why Joseph Martin might have decided to write a diary during this difficult experience. (to stave off boredom, to relieve loneliness, to help him remember the period in his life after the war was over)

Have students rewrite *Hard Times at Valley Forge* as a newspaper article. After students have completed their articles, have volunteers read them aloud to the class.

YAACOV'S JOURNEY

by Evelyn Wilde Mayerson
Pages 38–40

Use with Chapter 5, Lesson 3

Objectives

- ☐ *Recognize how difficult the immigration process could be for immigrants arriving at Ellis Island.*
- ☐ *Understand that passing inspection was important for Yaacov and his family.*
- ☐ *Dramatize Yaacov's Journey.*

Dramatizing the Story

After students have read the story, discuss it with them. Ask students why the inspector nearly prevented Yaacov from entering the United States. (Yaacov was deaf, and the United States did not usually allow people with handicaps or diseases to enter.) Ask students: *Why did the inspector change his mind about Yaacov?* (When Yaacov identified what the inspector had eaten for breakfast, the inspector realized that being handicapped did not mean that Yaacov was not quick-thinking and intelligent.)

Have students dramatize "Yaacov's Journey." Choose volunteers to play the parts of the main characters—Yaacov, Chanah, Raizel, the inspector, and the interpreter. Choose one student to be the narrator to read the descriptive parts of the selection. The rest of the class might take the parts of the other immigrants. Encourage students to familiarize themselves with their lines before performing the dramatization.

IN THE YEAR OF THE BOAR AND JACKIE ROBINSON

by Bette Bao Lord
Pages 41–46

Use with Chapter 5, Lesson 3

Objectives

❑ *Identify the difficulties faced by new immigrants like Shirley Temple Wong.*

❑ *Recognize that despite the problems they confront, many people still choose to immigrate to the United States.*

Background Information

Help students to understand that the phrase "year of the boar" refers to the Chinese calendar. Each of the 12 years of the Chinese calendar is referred to by a different animal name: rat, ox, tiger, hare, dragon, snake, horse, sheep, monkey, rooster, dog, and pig (or boar). The year 1947 was the year of the boar.

Linking to Today

After students have read the selection, ask them to list the difficulties that Shirley Temple Wong experienced in her first year in the United States. (language problems, teasing from her classmates for being the "teacher's pet," unfamiliarity with American customs) Discuss with students the connection between Shirley Temple Wong and Jackie Robinson. (Robinson overcame hostility and injustice to excell and make a change; Wong felt isolated and confused in her adopted culture.)

Students should realize that although the story about Shirley Temple Wong takes place in 1947, it describes problems faced by immigrants today. Have students write a paragraph explaining why many immigrants find it worthwhile to face these challenges. Ask volunteers to share their responses with the class.

Students might enjoy reading the book, *In the Year of the Boar and Jackie Robinson*, which is available in the Classroom Library.

THE CRICKET IN TIMES SQUARE

by George Selden
Pages 47–51

Use with Chapter 6, Lesson 2

Objectives

❑ *Recognize that crickets are not commonly found in New York City.*

❑ *Understand why the cricket was so important to Mario.*

❑ *Rewrite the selection from the cricket's perspective.*

Exploring Perspectives

After students have read the selection, ask volunteers to recall what Mario did when he found the cricket. (He held it as carefully as he could and then carried it back to the newsstand.) Ask students what the cricket did when Mario carried him back to the newsstand. (He didn't move or make a sound; he lay still, as if he were sleeping or frightened.)

Ask a volunteer to read aloud the paragraph in which Mario dusts off the cricket. Have students consider the cricket's reaction to this cleaning. Then have students reread the rest of the selection while considering the cricket's reaction.

Have students rewrite the selection from the cricket's perspective. Some students might enjoy illustrating their stories. After they have completed their stories and illustrations, ask volunteers to share them with the rest of the class.

CITY, CITY
by Marci Ridlon
Page 52 🔲

Use with Chapter 6, Lesson 2

Objectives

- ☐ *List the good things and the bad things about living in a city that are mentioned in this selection.*
- ☐ *Recognize that there are both good and bad things about living in most places.*
- ☐ *Write a poem describing some of the good and the bad things about living in your community.*

Writing Your Own Poem

After students have read the poem, play it for them on the cassette. After they have listened to the poem, ask volunteers to read it aloud. Discuss with students why the poet might have chosen to write the poem in two columns, side by side.

Ask volunteers to describe some of the things they like about their community. Then ask them to describe some of the things they dislike. Have students write their own poems about their community. Suggest that they also write a poem in two columns. Have students illustrate their poems. Then ask volunteers to share their poems and illustrations with the class.

KNOXVILLE, TENNESSEE
by Nikki Giovanni
Page 54 🔲

Use with Chapter 7, Lessons 1 and 2

Objectives

- ☐ *Recognize the reasons that the poet likes summer best of all the seasons.*
- ☐ *Identify how Nikki Giovanni uses poetry to describe what summer means to her.*
- ☐ *Write a poem about one of the seasons.*

Writing Your Own Poem

After students have read the poem, play it for them on the cassette. After listening to the poem, volunteers might enjoy reading it aloud to the class. Discuss with students why they think Nikki Giovanni chose to write a poem about the summer. Have students imagine that the poem has no title. Ask students: *What elements from the poem might help you determine which region the poem is written about?* (fresh corn, okra, gospel music, mountains, warm climate year-round) Ask volunteers to tell which seasons are most special for them. Ask questions such as: *What do you like to do during your favorite season? How does the geography of our region affect the activities you do during each season?*

Then have students write poems about their favorite seasons and illustrate them. Make a bulletin board display of the poems around the title, "Our Favorite Seasons."

WHEN I WAS YOUNG IN THE MOUNTAINS

by Cynthia Rylant
Pages 55–57

Use with Chapter 7, Lesson 1

Objectives

❑ *Identify some of Cynthia Rylant's memories of living in the mountains.*

❑ *Recognize how the use of repetition affects the story.*

❑ *Write a story about everyday life.*

Writing Your Own Story

After students have read the selection, discuss with them the things that the author remembered about her everyday life as a child in the mountains. Have volunteers read aloud their favorite paragraphs from the selection. Then ask volunteers to tell about everyday things that were special to them when they were younger. Encourage students to think about their everyday lives and to compare them with the author's childhood memories.

Have students write a story called *When I Was Young in _____*. Suggest that students begin each paragraph with the phrase, "When I was young in _____." After students have completed their stories, ask volunteers to read them to the class.

JOHN HENRY

Traditional Ballad
Pages 58–59

Use with Chapter 7, Lesson 2

Objectives

❑ *Recognize that during the 1870s machines started to replace men in building railroads.*

❑ *Understand the origin of John Henry, the folk hero.*

❑ *Create a poster about John Henry.*

Creating a Poster

After students have read the lyrics to the song, play Paul Robeson's performance of the ballad for them on the cassette. Discuss the lyrics of the song with the class verse by verse. Ask students: *What did John Henry mean when he said, "This hammer'll be the death of me, Lord, Lord . . ."?* (that he would die from working with a hammer) *Who was the captain and why did he say, "I'm gonna bring that steam drill around . . ."?* (the man in charge of building the railroad, who was bringing a machine to do some of the work) *What did John Henry tell the captain?* ("A man ain't nothing but a man . . . .") *What happened to John Henry in the next verse?* (In trying to prove that he could do as much as a machine, he worked so hard that he died.) *What do the trains say as they pass John Henry's grave?* ("There lies a steel-driving man.")

Have students draw posters about John Henry. Divide the class into five groups, one for each of the verses. Have each group draw a poster to represent one of the verses. After students have completed their posters, display them on the bulletin board.

GO FREE OR DIE

by Jerri Ferris
Pages 60–63

Use with Chapter 8, Lesson 2

Objectives

- ❑ *Identify the meaning of the Underground Railroad.*
- ❑ *Recognize Harriet Tubman's experience with the Underground Railroad.*
- ❑ *Perform "Go Free or Die" as Story Theater.*

Using Story Theater

After students have finished reading the selection, ask volunteers to share their reactions to Harriet Tubman's experiences. Encourage students to talk about her fears as described in the biography. Ask students to explain why many people called Harriet Tubman "Moses." (because, like Moses in the Bible, Tubman led her people to freedom)

Have students perform the selection in a Story Theater. Choose volunteers to play the parts of the main characters—Harriet, Mr. Trent, and Thomas Garrett. Choose one student as narrator to read the descriptive parts of the selection. Several students might take the parts of the slave catchers, the guards, and the two horsemen. Suggest that Harriet's character might use a man's hat and a hat with a veil to indicate change of costume. Encourage students to familiarize themselves with their lines before the performance.

Students might enjoy reading all of *Go Free or Die: The Story of Harriet Tubman*, which is available in the Classroom Library.

THE RIDDLE TALE OF FREEDOM

by Virginia Hamilton
Pages 64–65

Use with Chapter 8, Lesson 2

Objectives

- ❑ *Identify the origin of riddle tales.*
- ❑ *Appreciate how riddle tales expressed hope for freedom by enslaved African Americans.*
- ❑ *Write a riddle tale.*

Writing Your Own Riddle Tale

After students have read the selection, discuss riddle tales with them. Encourage students to recognize that riddle tales were a source of symbolic freedom for enslaved African Americans. Ask volunteers to share other riddles with the class.

Have students write their own riddle tales about something that is important to them. After students have completed their riddle tales, have volunteers share the tales with the rest of the class.

BATTLE CRY OF FREEDOM
Civil War Battle Songs
Pages 66–67

Use with Chapter 8, Lesson 3

Objectives

❑ *Identify the perspective revealed in the lyrics to the Northern version of the popular Civil War song "Battle Cry of Freedom."*

❑ *Identify the perspective revealed in the lyrics to the Southern version of "Battle Cry of Freedom."*

❑ *Write an essay about the different perspectives of the North and the South during the Civil War.*

Exploring Perspectives

After students have read the lyrics of the songs, play the songs for them on the cassette. Ask volunteers to describe how the songs are alike. (same melody and harmony) Ask students: *How are they different?* (different lyrics) Have students find differences in the lyrics. (Union/Dixie, up with the star/up with the cross, and although he may be poor he shall never be a slave/their motto is resistance—"To tyrants we'll not yield!") Discuss the differences between the North and the South as expressed in the songs.

Have students write a short essay on the different perspectives that the people of the North and the people of the South had during the Civil War. After students have completed their essays, ask volunteers to read them to the class.

ROSA PARKS: MY STORY
by Rosa Parks
Pages 68–69

Use with Chapter 9, Lesson 2

Objectives

❑ *Recognize the importance of Rosa Parks's refusal to give up her seat on a bus.*

❑ *Identify how reading Rosa Parks's own words helps to better understand the event.*

❑ *Write a newspaper article about the events described in Rosa Parks: My Story.*

Rewriting in Another Genre

After students have read the excerpt from *Rosa Parks: My Story*, have volunteers read the selection aloud. Ask students to identify the parts of the story that only Rosa Parks knows. (the many places where she describes her thoughts and feelings) Ask students why Rosa Parks finally wrote her own story about the events of December 1955. (probably, to finally tell the details correctly)

Have students rewrite *Rosa Parks: My Story* as a newspaper article. Remind students of the five Ws— the *Who, What, When, Where,* and *Why.* Suggest that in their articles students interview the bus driver and other passengers on the bus. After students have completed their articles, ask volunteers to read them to the rest of the class.

I SEE THE PROMISED LAND

by Martin Luther King, Jr.
Pages 70–71 🔲

Use with Chapter 9, Lesson 2

Objectives

- ☐ *Recognize Martin Luther King's leadership in the civil rights movement.*
- ☐ *Describe the effect of Martin Luther King's speech, "I See the Promised Land."*
- ☐ *Write a response to the question, "Have we reached King's 'promised land' yet?"*

Linking to Today

After students have read the speech, play it for them on the cassette. Tell students that they are listening to Martin Luther King, Jr., speaking his own words. Ask students to describe how King's words affected them. Discuss the difference between the effect of reading the speech and hearing it on the cassette. Ask students what King meant by the "promised land." (a place and time when racial harmony would be achieved)

Have students write a short essay in response to the question, "Have we reached King's 'promised land' yet?" When students have completed their essays, ask volunteers to share them with the class.

I HEAR AMERICA SINGING

by Walt Whitman
Page 72 🔲

I, TOO

by Langston Hughes
Page 73 🔲

Use with Chapter 9, Lesson 2

Objectives

- ☐ *Identify how Walt Whitman uses poetry to describe his view of America.*
- ☐ *Identify how Langston Hughes uses poetry to describe his hopes for African Americans.*
- ☐ *Write a poem linking both poems to America today.*

Linking to Today

After students have read each poem, play them on the cassette. Share with students that they are hearing Langston Hughes read his own poem. After listening to the poems, volunteers might want to read the poems aloud to the class. Discuss with students the people and workers referred to in Whitman's poem. (mechanics, carpenter, mason, boatman, and so on) Ask students to identify the line in Hughes's poem that shows it was written in response to Whitman's. ("I, too, sing America.") Ask students why they think Hughes felt the need to write a response. (because Whitman had written about ordinary people, but not people who were sent to the kitchen to eat)

Have students listen again to the Hughes recording. Remind them that they are listening to Langston Hughes reading his own poem. Ask them to listen for a difference between the written and the recorded versions of the poem. (Hughes says, "They'll see how beautiful we are." The poem is written, "They'll see how beautiful I am.") Ask students: *Why do you think Hughes changed the words? Which version do you prefer?*

Have students write a poem about America today. Encourage them to write about what they hear America singing. Students might enjoy illustrating their poems. After students have completed their poems, ask volunteers to read them to the rest of the class.

PUERTO RICO
by Eileen Figueroa
Page 74

Use with Chapter 9, Lesson 2

Objectives
- ❏ *Recognize how Eileen Figueroa expresses her love for Puerto Rico through poetry.*
- ❏ *Write a poem about a special place.*

Writing Your Own Poem

After students have read the poem, play it for them on the cassette. After listening to the poem in Spanish and English, volunteers might want to read aloud both versions to the class. Discuss with students why Eileen Figueroa might have chosen to express herself through poetry. (Poetry is often used to express beauty and emotion.) Ask students: *What special features about Puerto Rico does Figueroa describe?* (its beauty, its palms, and its sea breezes) *How does she describe the evenings on the island?* (calming and serene with coquies singing in the distance)

Ask volunteers to tell about a place that is special to them. Ask such questions as: *What about the place makes it special? Is it the sights? Is it the sounds? Is it the people?* Have students write their own poems about a place that is special to them. Students might enjoy illustrating their poems. Create a book of poems titled *My Special Place.*

HEARTLAND
by Diane Siebert
Pages 76–79

Use with Chapter 10, Lesson 1

Objectives
- ❏ *Recognize why Diane Siebert calls the Middle West the "heartland."*
- ❏ *Identify how Diane Siebert uses poetry to celebrate the farmers and their land.*
- ❏ *Write a poem about students' own region.*

Writing Your Own Poem

After students have read the poem, play it for them on the cassette. After they have listened to the poem, ask volunteers to read it aloud. Discuss with students why they think that Diane Siebert uses the word *heartland* to describe the Middle West. (because the region produces much of the food that feeds the people of the United States; because the Middle West is geographically at the center of, or at the heart of, the United States; Remind students that their hearts feed blood to their bodies.) Have students imagine that the poem has no title. Ask students: *How would you identify the region that this poem describes?* (fields of grain, blizzards, giant mills, stockyards, wheat fields, cornfields, and the many references to farms and farmers) Have volunteers share features of their own region that make it special. Encourage students to brainstorm about their region. As students name examples, list them on chart paper or on the chalkboard.

Have each student write a poem about his or her region. Encourage students to think about the entire region and the changes that occur with the different seasons of the year. After students have completed their poems, have them draw illustrations to accompany them. Encourage volunteers to share their poems and illustrations with the class.

SARAH, PLAIN AND TALL
by Patricia MacLachlan
Pages 80–83

Use with Chapter 11, Lessons 1 and 3

Objectives

- ❏ *Recognize that many people moved from the Northeast to the Middle West during the 1800s.*
- ❏ *Identify how the story describes the differences between the Northeast and the Middle West during the 1800s.*
- ❏ *Perform* Sarah, Plain and Tall *as Readers Theatre.*

Using Readers Theatre

After students have read the story, discuss with them their reactions to Sarah's move from the Northeast to the Middle West. Ask students: *What are some of the memories and souvenirs that Sarah brought with her from the Northeast?* (the shells on her windowsill, memories of her home and family, a song) Have students imagine that they have moved to a region far away from their own. Ask volunteers to name some of the things about their region that they would miss. As students name examples, write them on chart paper or on the chalkboard.

Have students perform *Sarah, Plain and Tall* as Readers Theatre. Choose volunteers to take the parts of the main characters—Sarah, Anna, Caleb, Papa. Remind students that in Readers Theatre they do not move about, but try to read with expression. Encourage students to familiarize themselves with their parts before the performance.

Students might enjoy reading the book, *Sarah, Plain and Tall*, which is available in the Classroom Library.

TRUE STORIES ABOUT ABRAHAM LINCOLN
by Ruth Belov Gross
Pages 84–86

Use with Chapter 11, Lesson 1

Objectives

- ❏ *Identify how the stories describe some of the qualities that helped Abraham Lincoln to become a strong leader.*
- ❏ *Draw a poster illustrating a story about Abraham Lincoln.*

Creating Posters

After students have read the stories, ask them to tell what they learned about Lincoln's personality from each of the stories. (He was honest, responsible, hard-working, clever, and practical.)

Divide the class into three groups, one for each story. Have each group draw a poster to represent its story about Abe Lincoln. After students have completed their posters, display them on the bulletin board titled "Honest Abe."

THE BUFFALO GO
by Old Lady Horse
Pages 87–88

Use with Chapter 11, Traditions

BUFFALO DUSK
by Carl Sandburg
Page 89 📼

Use with Chapter 11, Lesson 2

Objectives

❑ *Recognize how the legend makes clear the importance of the buffalo to the Kiowa.*

❑ *Recognize how Carl Sandburg expresses his sadness over the loss of the buffalo through poetry.*

❑ *Compare and contrast the perspectives of the Kiowa and some whites.*

Exploring Perspectives

After students have read the legend and the poem, play the poem for them on the cassette. Tell students that they are listening to Carl Sandburg reading his own poem. Then discuss the selections with them. Ask volunteers to describe the reasons that the buffalo were important to the Kiowa. (They were sacrificed in the Sun Dance and used in the Kiowa's prayers; hides were used to make clothing and tepees; meat was used for food; bladders and stomachs were made into containers.) Ask students: *How did the buffalo become extinct?* (Too many were killed.) *Why did some white people kill the buffalo?* (to make room for railroads, farms, and ranches; to sell the hides; to force the Indians onto reservations)

Have students discuss the different perspectives of the Kiowa and some whites toward the buffalo. Ask students: *Do you think that the perspective of the white hunters might be different today?* (Probably; because today there is more understanding and respect for other cultures.) Have students consider Carl Sandburg's perspective toward the buffalo. Point out that Sandburg was a white man who was saddened by the loss of the buffalo.

Have students write a short essay on the different perspectives of the Kiowa and some whites during the late 1800s. After students have completed their essays, ask volunteers to read them aloud.

MY PRAIRIE YEAR
by Brett Harvey
Pages 90–93

Use with Chapter 11, Lesson 3

Objectives

❑ *Describe the daily life of Elenore Plaisted on the prairie in 1889.*

❑ *Draw a storyboard with captions that describes daily life on the prairie.*

Drawing Storyboards with Captions

After students have read the selection, discuss with them the image of Elenore's house as described by Brett Harvey. ("a little white ship at sea, surrounded by endless tall grass that billowed in the wind like the waves of an ocean") Then ask students: *What did Elenore do on each day of the week?* (Monday–washing; Tuesday–ironing, mending, and sewing; Wednesday–gardening and lessons; Thursday–shopping; Friday–cleaning; Saturday–cooking and baking; Sunday–running free)

Divide the class into seven groups, one for each day of the week. Have each group write a list of Elenore's activities for its assigned day. Then have each group draw a storyboard that illustrates the activities and write a caption for it. After the storyboards have been completed, display them on the bulletin board.

LIFE ON THE PRAIRIE WITH THE INGALLS FAMILY

Pages 94–95

Use with Chapter 11, Lesson 3

Objectives

- ❑ *Identify the objects from Laura Ingalls Wilder's life on the prairie.*
- ❑ *Recognize the importance of objects from the past.*
- ❑ *Create a montage of objects from students' lives.*

Creating a Montage

After students have looked at the artifacts, discuss the value of seeing real objects from the past. Ask students: *Why is it interesting to look at the original manuscript, the photograph, and the old newspaper?* (The objects help us to feel a connection with the author.)

Have students work together in groups to create a montage of objects from their own lives. Suggest that each group choose three objects that represent students' lives. Have them title the montage "Life in [student's town]." When students have completed the montage, display it on the bulletin board.

THE WABASH CANNONBALL

by A. P. Carter
Page 96

Use with Chapter 11, Lesson 3

Objectives

- ❑ *Identify the significance of the song "The Wabash Cannonball."*
- ❑ *Create a poster about the Wabash Cannonball.*

Creating Posters

After students have read the lyrics to the song, play it for them on the cassette. Ask students: *Why do you think that the train was called the Cannonball?* (because it rumbled, roared, and echoed down the valley like a cannonball) *Where did the Wabash Cannonball travel?* (from California to Labrador, with stops in St. Paul, Kansas City, Des Moines, and Kankakee) Help students to locate Labrador on a map of Canada. Have students trace the route on a map of the United States.

Have students draw posters to encourage people to ride the Wabash Cannonball. Encourage students to use images from the song for their posters. After students have completed their posters, display them on the bulletin board.

DOTY'S WASHER
Advertisement from the 1800s
Page 97

Use with Chapter 11, Lesson 3

Objectives

❑ *Recognize why housekeepers in the 1800s would prefer Doty's Washer to the old washboard.*

❑ *Design and create a poster for a new product that will improve people's lives.*

Creating Posters

After students have read the advertisement, ask a volunteer to read it aloud. Ask students why the advertisement might have appealed to women during the 1800s. (It promised to "save their money and clothes" while reducing their work by nearly half.)

Have students draw a poster showing an advertisement for a product of their choice. Suggest that students show an advertisement for today on the left side of the poster. On the right side of the poster, have students draw an advertisement for the future. Have students write advertising copy describing the products. Display the completed advertisements on the bulletin board.

FAMILY FARM
by Thomas Locker
Pages 98–102

WORKING THE LAND
by Pierce Walker
Pages 103–104

Use with Chapter 12, Lesson 2

Objectives

❑ *Identify the perspectives of two farmers about their work.*

❑ *Compare and contrast the perspectives of the two farmers about their work.*

Exploring Perspectives

After students have read the selections, discuss their reactions to them. Ask students to describe the ways in which the two selections are similar. (Both are about the difficulties of farming.) Then ask students to describe the ways in which the two selections are different. (*Working the Land* is about a large farm on which machinery plays a major part. *Family Farm* is about a small farm on which the work done by family members continues to be very important.)

Have students write a short essay on the different perspectives that the two farmers have about farming. After students have completed their essays, ask volunteers to read them to the class.

THE ERRAND

by Harry Behn
Page 106

Use with Chapter 13, Lesson 1

Objectives

- ☐ *Identify some of the geographical features of the southwestern region of the United States.*
- ☐ *Recognize why Harry Behn described his errand through poetry.*
- ☐ *Draw a storyboard with captions for a video.*

Drawing Storyboards with Captions

After students have read the poem, play it for them on the cassette. After listening to the poem, volunteers might want to read it aloud to the class. Direct students' attention to the different images described in each of the verses. (a trip by pony to a faraway farm, a water tank on top of a hill, a windmill bringing up rusty water, a graveyard overgrown with gourds and grass, a valley with one house and one tree, a book left inside an empty house, the setting sun and the rising moon) Ask volunteers to tell why they think Harry Behn chose to write about his errand in the form of a poem. (The journey to the neighboring farm was full of visual surprises; the poet is sensitive to beauty.)

Divide the class into seven groups, one for each of the poem's verses. Have one group draw a storyboard for each verse to plan a video of the poem. Then have each group write a caption for its storyboard. After the storyboards have been completed, display them on the bulletin board.

I'M IN CHARGE OF CELEBRATIONS

by Byrd Baylor
Pages 107–108

Use with Chapter 13, Lesson 2

Objectives

- ☐ *Identify how Byrd Baylor uses poetry to describe her New Year's celebration.*
- ☐ *Identify some geographical features of the Southwest.*
- ☐ *Write a poem about a New Year's celebration.*

Writing Your Own Poem

After students have read the poem to themselves, ask volunteers to read it aloud to the class. Then ask students such questions as: *Why does the narrator of the poem celebrate the new year at the beginning of spring?* (She never felt that her new year started on January 1; spring is when the narrator feels that the new year truly begins.) Suggest that students skim the poem to find the signs of spring that Byrd Baylor celebrates. *How does she spend the day she celebrates as New Year's day?* (admiring things) *With whom does she celebrate?* (horned toads, ravens, lizards, and quail) *Which things mentioned in the poem suggest that it is set in the Southwest?* (cactus, desert, horned toad, lizards, tortoises)

Have students think about what time of year they would choose to celebrate the new year. Then have students write a poem about that celebration. Suggest to students that they write their poems in a style similar to that of "I'm in Charge of Celebrations." Tell students to illustrate their poems. Then have volunteers share their poems and illustrations with the class.

PUEBLO STORYTELLER
by Diane Hoyt-Goldsmith
Pages 109–111

Use with Chapter 14, Lesson 1

Objectives

- ☐ *Recognize that storytelling is an important tradition among the Pueblo people.*
- ☐ *Recognize how April has become a storyteller.*
- ☐ *Perform "How the People Came to Earth" as Story Theater.*

Using Story Theater

After students have read the selection, discuss it with them. Ask students to name some of the subjects of the stories that April's grandparents told her. (legends of the Pueblo people; things that happened in their own lives) Ask students: *Which time of year was the subject of the story that was told to April by her grandmother?* (autumn) *What activities was the family involved in during autumn?* (harvesting and husking corn) *Which legend did April's grandparents tell her?* ("How the People Came to Earth")

Have students perform the selection in a Story Theater. Choose students for the parts of the narrator, the mole, and Old Spider Woman. Several students can represent the people. Encourage students to familiarize themselves with the story before staging the performance.

GIT ALONG, LITTLE DOGIES
American Cowboy Song
Pages 112–113

Use with Chapter 14, Lesson 3

Objectives

- ☐ *Understand why cowboys sang songs on cattle drives.*
- ☐ *Write a new verse to the song, "Git Along, Little Dogies."*

Writing Your Own Verse to a Song

After students have read the lyrics to the song, play it for them on the cassette. Point out to students that the written words differ slightly from the words on the cassette. Tell them that the song is a traditional one with many variations. Discuss with students why cowboys might have sung on the cattle drives. (to pass the time, to entertain themselves) Remind students that cowboys worked day after day, eating and sleeping outdoors. Ask students what the word *dogies* refers to in the song. (motherless or stray calves) Ask students: *Why do you think the cowboys sometimes sang to the cattle and the dogies?* (The words to the song were the cowboys' way of talking to the cattle and the dogies.)

Have students write a fourth verse to the song. Remind students to try to use rhyming words at the ends of the second and fourth lines. When students have completed their verses, have them draw accompanying illustrations. Encourage volunteers to share their verses and illustrations with the class.

KATE HEADS WEST

by Pat Brisson
Pages 114–117

Use with Chapter 15, Lesson 1

Objectives

☐ *Identify some of the geographical attractions found in the Southwest as described in the selection.*

☐ *Draw postcards illustrating attractions of the Southwest.*

Drawing Your Own Postcards

After students have read the selection, discuss each postcard with them. Ask students to imagine what picture might be shown on the first postcard. (a rodeo in Fort Worth) Suggest that students skim the message on the first postcard to find clues about the picture. Then ask students: *What pictures might be on the other postcards?* (the desert; the Rio Grande or Juarez; Gila Cliff Dwellings National Monument; the Petrified Forest; the Grand Canyon)

Divide the class into six groups. Have each group draw one postcard. Suggest that students reread Kate's message for possible images to use in their illustrations. After students have completed their postcards display them on a bulletin board titled "Postcards from the Southwest."

THE TEXAS SPIRIT

by Barbara Jordan
Pages 118–119

Use with Chapter 15, Lesson 1

Objectives

☐ *Identify important events in Barbara Jordan's life as described in the interview.*

☐ *Recognize some of Barbara Jordan's personal strengths.*

☐ *Write an essay about Barbara Jordan.*

Writing Your Own Essay

After students have read the interview with Barbara Jordan, discuss the selection. Ask volunteers to share their reactions to Jordan's life as described in the interview. Encourage students to talk about Jordan's response to the obstacles she met. (She decided to change things.) Ask a volunteer to read aloud the paragraph that describes what Jordan's father taught her. Finally ask a volunteer to read aloud what Jordan says about Texas.

Have students reread the selection and write a few sentences that summarize each paragraph. Tell students to use their sentences as a guideline for a brief essay about Barbara Jordan. After students have completed their essays, have volunteers read them to the class.

JUSTIN AND THE BEST BISCUITS IN THE WORLD
by Mildred Pitts Walter
Pages 120–125

Use with Chapter 15, Lesson 1

Objectives

- ☐ *Identify Justin's point of view about work.*
- ☐ *Identify Grandpa's point of view about work.*
- ☐ *Write an essay.*

Exploring Perspectives

After students have read the selection, have them discuss Justin's view of "man's work." Ask students: *What did Justin expect to learn on his visit to the ranch?* ("man's work") *Why was Justin surprised when Grandpa took the utensils from the shed?* (He hadn't expected Grandpa to cook.) *What did Justin learn about cooking from Grandpa?* (that some of the best cooks in the world are men)

On the chalkboard or chart paper write *Grandpa* and *Justin.* Ask students to skim the selection for examples that illustrate the points of view of both Grandpa and Justin on the subject of work. Ask students to volunteer the examples that they find and write them under the appropriate name.

Have students write a list of the chores they do at home. Then have students write an essay about their own points of view on the subject of men's work and women's work. After students have completed their essays, ask volunteers to read them aloud to the class.

AN APACHE GIRL BECOMES A WOMAN
by Telly Declay
Pages 127–130

Use with Chapter 15, Lesson 2

Objectives

- ☐ *Recognize the importance of the Sunrise Dance.*
- ☐ *Identify some features of the Sunrise Dance.*
- ☐ *Write a description of a ceremony.*

Background Information

The *Daybreak Star* is a newspaper that publishes articles written by Native American students throughout the United States. Telly Declay was 12 years old in 1982 when she wrote "An Apache Girl Becomes a Woman." She hopes to become an artist.

Writing About a Ceremony

After students have read Telly's description of the Sunrise Dance and her preparation for it, have them discuss the importance of the Sunrise Dance. (The ceremony will help her to be strong and to live long.) Encourage volunteers to tell which part of the ceremony they think is most important. Then ask a volunteer to read aloud the last paragraph of the selection. Encourage students to tell why they think Telly wrote "An Apache Girl Becomes a Woman."

Ask volunteers to describe ceremonies with which they are familiar that celebrate the passage from childhood into adulthood. Then have students write a description of a ceremony. Some students might write about an imaginary ceremony in which they would enjoy participating. After students have completed their descriptions, ask volunteers to read them aloud to the class.

SIERRA

by Diane Siebert
Pages 132–135 🔲

Use with Chapter 16, Lessons 1 and 2

Objectives

☐ *Recognize how Diane Siebert used poetry to describe the history of the Sierra Mountains.*

☐ *Recognize some of the changes in the history of the Sierra Mountains.*

☐ *Write a letter to Diane Siebert.*

Writing a Letter

After students have read the poem silently, play it for them on the cassette. Then ask volunteers to read the poem aloud. Discuss with students why Diane Siebert might have chosen to write a poem about the Sierras. Point out to students that Siebert describes changes that have taken place in the mountains over millions of years. Ask students to skim the poem to find some of these changes. Then ask a volunteer to read the last stanza of the poem. Discuss with students the meaning of Siebert's warning that the mountains depend on how man cares for them.

Have students write a letter to Diane Siebert describing how people can take care of the mountains. After students have completed their letters, have volunteers read theirs to the class. Encourage students to mail their letters to Siebert.

ROLL ON, COLUMBIA

by Woody Guthrie
Pages 136–137 🔲

Use with Chapter 16, Lesson 2

Objectives

☐ *Recognize how Woody Guthrie's song conveys the beauty and importance of the Columbia River.*

☐ *Identify the route of the Columbia River.*

Tracing a Route

After students have read the lyrics to the song, play it for them on the cassette. Students may enjoy singing along with the cassette. Tell students that they are listening to Woody Guthrie sing his own song. Discuss with students why Woody Guthrie wrote a song about the Columbia River and electric power. Point out to students that the hydroelectric power from the Columbia River brought electricity to millions of people.

Have students trace the route of the Columbia River on a map of North America. Ask questions such as: *The Columbia River forms part of the border of which two states?* (Oregon and Washington) *Through what mountain ranges does it flow?* (Coast Ranges, Cascade Range) *In what other country does the Columbia River flow?* (Canada)

ARCTIC MEMORIES
by Normee Ekoomiak
Pages 138–140

Use with Chapter 17, Lesson 1

Objectives

- ❏ *Identify Normee Ekoomiak's memories of Inuit survival in the snow and ice.*
- ❏ *Recognize how Normee Ekoomiak keeps Inuit traditions alive through his writing and art.*
- ❏ *Create posters of Arctic life.*

Creating a Poster

After students have read the selection, discuss it with them. Ask volunteers to describe some of Normee Ekoomiak's memories about how the Inuits lived with the cold. (They lived in snow houses and slept in large groups to keep warm.) Point out to students that Ekoomiak designed the illustration that accompanies the selection. Discuss with students how Ekoomiak has adapted to his new environment.

Have students choose one paragraph in the selection to illustrate in a poster. Display students' posters on the bulletin board titled "Arctic Memories."

WHEN THE WIND BLOWS HARD
by Denise Gosliner Orenstein
Pages 141–144

Use with Chapter 17, Lesson 1

Objectives

- ❏ *Recognize some of the characteristics that Shawn learned about Tlingit culture.*
- ❏ *Identify some forms of Tlingit art.*
- ❏ *Write a biography of Vesta's grandfather.*

Writing a Biography

After students have read the story, discuss it with them. Ask volunteers to describe what Shawn learned about woodcarving during her visit with Vesta's grandfather. (Carving is an art that is treated as something alive and respected.) Then ask volunteers to describe what Shawn learned about the Tlingit's totem poles. (A symbolic animal is on top; people paint the poles while the poles are lying on the ground.) Ask volunteers to describe the totem pole animals. (The fox, the crab, and the mosquito represent a child, a thief, and teaching, respectively.) Ask students to describe what Shawn learned about the Tlingit and gifts. (The Tlingit never refuse a gift, but accept it with open arms.)

Have students write a short biography of Vesta's grandfather based on the information they have read in the selection. Suggest that students illustrate their biographies with drawings of Vesta's grandfather's carving or totem pole. Have volunteers read their biographies to the rest of the class.

BY THE GREAT HORN SPOON!

by Sid Fleischman
Pages 145–147

Use with Chapter 17, Lesson 3

Objectives

- ☐ *Recognize why Jack and Praiseworthy went to California during the mid-1800s.*
- ☐ *Recognize some of the hardships of mining camps during the Gold Rush.*
- ☐ *Perform a Readers Theatre of* By the Great Horn Spoon!

Using Readers Theatre

After students have read the selection discuss it with them. Ask students to describe how Jack and Praiseworthy were typical of other Forty-Niners. (They went to California to get rich quick and then leave.) Then ask students what Jack and Praiseworthy had learned by the end of the story. (that getting rich quick was not going to be as easy as they hoped)

Have students perform *By the Great Horn Spoon!* as Readers Theatre. The selection gives students an opportunity to read dialogue and some interesting vocabulary. Choose students to take the parts of Jack, Praiseworthy, the waiter, the miner, and the narrator. Several students might take the parts of other miners in the camp. Encourage students to familiarize themselves with their lines before the performance.

THE HEAVY PANTS OF MR. STRAUSS

by June Swanson
Pages 148–149

Use with Chapter 17, Lesson 3

Objectives

- ☐ *Identify the advantages of Levi's as shown in the advertisement.*
- ☐ *Recognize why Levi Strauss invented blue jeans*
- ☐ *Create an advertisement.*

Creating an Advertisement

After students have read the essay, discuss it with them. Ask volunteers to explain the connection between the California Gold Rush and the invention of blue jeans. (The miners needed pants tough enough to stand up against rocks and the hard mining life.) Ask students: *What is the origin of the word* denim? (de Nimes [nēm]) *What is the origin of the word* Levi's? (Levi Strauss)

Have students look at the advertisement that accompanies this essay. Point out the two horses pulling the Levi's in opposite directions. Ask volunteers to describe the meaning of the ad. (It emphasizes the strength and toughness of the fabric.) Then ask volunteers to describe in what way today's ads differ from the ad shown with the essay. (Today's ads focus on Levi's for leisure-wear.) Point out to students that today the Levi's logo is widely recognized.

Have students draw an original advertisement for blue jeans. Suggest to students that they think about when and how they wear their blue jeans. Encourage them to draw an imaginative advertisement. Display students' completed advertisements on the bulletin board titled "Blue Jeans Today."

HECTOR LIVES IN THE UNITED STATES NOW
by Joan Hewett
Pages 150–154

Use with Chapter 18, Lesson 2

Objectives

❏ *Recognize some of the difficulties encountered by Hector Almaraz, a Mexican-American immigrant.*

❏ *Identify some of the important events in Hector's life.*

❏ *Draw a storyboard with captions.*

Drawing Storyboards with Captions

After students have read the selection, have them identify the problem that Hector faced when he started kindergarten. (He could not understand or speak English.) Have students suggest other problems that immigrants to the United States typically face. (lack of familiarity with customs, loneliness, economic hardship, and so on) Then have students compare and contrast Hector's life in the United States with their own.

Have 10 groups of students prepare storyboards from *Hector Lives in the United States Now* to plan a video. Ask each group of students to draw a scene that represents one of the following parts of the selection. 1. Hector's family; 2. Hector and his friends playing games; 3. Hector and his friends on the front stoop; 4. Hector and his brother at the kitchen table; 5. Hector in kindergarten; 6. Hector in fifth grade; 7. Philip, Nicky, Vanessa, Erick, Julie, Kyria, and Hector with their ancestors; 8. Hector working on a computer at the library; 9. Hector reading at home; 10. Hector and his family going to Mexico. Have students write captions for their storyboards. After students have completed the storyboards, make a display of them on a bulletin board.

THE FUN THEY HAD
by Isaac Asimov
Pages 155–158

Use with Chapter 18, Lesson 2

Objectives

❏ *Recognize that Isaac Asimov predicted the popular use of computers.*

❏ *Identify some of the differences between schools of the future and schools of today as described in* The Fun They Had.

❏ *Continue the diary entry.*

Continuing the Diary Entry

After students have read the story, discuss it with them. Then ask students to discuss the differences between Margie's school and schools of the past. Encourage students to consider what school would be like without other students or teachers. Suggest that students imagine what it would be like to attend school at home with only a television as a teacher. Ask students: *What information about schools long ago was surprising to Margie?* (that the teacher was a man; that students went to a school building; that students learned the same things) *How did Margie feel about her school?* (She hated it.)

Have students imagine that they are Margie and that they are to continue the diary entry, "Today Tommy found a real book!" Suggest that students express the feelings Margie might have had about paper books and schools with many children. After students have completed their diary entries, ask volunteers to read them aloud.

THE ALPINE SONG

Page 159 🔲

Use with Chapter 18, Building Bridges

Objectives

- 🔲 *Recognize that yodeling is associated with mountainous areas.*
- 🔲 *Write a verse to "The Alpine Song."*

Writing Your Own Verse

After students have read the lyrics to the song, play it for them on the cassette. Then play the song again and have the class sing along. Discuss with students why shepherds might have started yodeling in the mountains. Remind students that shepherds spend weeks alone tending their sheep. Shepherds called their sheep and kept them together by yodeling. The shepherds might have made up new verses to amuse themselves.

Have students write their own verses for "The Alpine Song." Encourage them to imagine animals, things, or events that might be found in a mountainous area. Suggest that each student write two new verses for the song. Students might enjoy creating a mountain-theme bulletin board on which they can display their songs. Other students might enjoy illustrating the song. Have volunteers sing their new verses for the class.

TEACHER'S NOTES

TEACHER'S NOTES

TEACHER'S NOTES

TEACHER'S NOTES